Mi Librito de Español

A Quick Reference Guide to Spanish Grammar for Students

MICHELLE "PROFE" TIEMAN

PROFE TIEMAN LLC

WINDHAM, NEW HAMPSHIRE

Mi Librito de Español
Copyright © 2021 by Michelle Tieman

Special discounts are available to school programs and educators seeking to purchase this resource in large quantities.

Published by Profe Tieman LLC
Windham, NH
www.profetieman.com

Cover Photo: iStockPhoto.com
Interior Clipart: Friendlystock.com
Profe Tieman Illustrations:

 Allison Sharpe Graphic Design

Edited by: Ivy Levine and Marisa Lerner-Lam

ISBN: 978-0-578-24686-4

Printed by: Wharf Industries in Windham, NH
April, 2021

First Edition

Dear Spanish Learner,

This booklet was designed with you in mind. With the help of my colleagues, I have compiled many of the grammar concepts that are taught from levels 1 through 5 in this comprehensive quick reference guide. Whether you are a first year student or a fifth year, this grammar guide will help you to master some of the most difficult grammar concepts such as ser vs estar, por vs para and so much more. Not sure what verb tense you need? Simply turn to page 15 and use the English translations as a guide to navigate this book with ease without needing to resort to unreliable resources such as translation apps. This book has been a game changer for my students and has helped them to increase their confidence and performance in Spanish. I hope that you too enjoy this resource and find it to be a useful tool as you embark on the beautiful journey of Spanish language learning. ¡Buena suerte!

Sincerely,

Profe Tieman

Table of Contents

************** Verb Tenses **************

Indicative Mood
(Past, Present, Future, Conditional)

Used to express actions or ideas that *indicate* something real or concrete such as facts, habitual actions, routines, etc. Exception: The Condition Tense is used for hypothetical situations.

Table of contents continued ➡

Table of Contents Continued
********* Verb Tenses Continued *********

Useful Resources

(Getting Started)

102 Common Spanish Verbs

abrir	to open	estudiar	to study	poder*	can/to be able to
acabar	to finish	existir	to exist	poner**	to put/place/set
aceptar	to accept	explicar	to explain	preferir*	to prefer
alcanzar	to reach/catch up	formar	to form	preguntar	to ask a question
aparecer	to appear	ganar	to win	presentar	to present/introduce
ayudar	to help	gustar	to be pleasing/like	producir	to produce/cause
buscar	to look for	haber	to have + past participle	quedar	to remain/stay
caer**	to fall	hablar	to talk/speak	querer*	to want/love
cambiar	to change	hacer**	to do/make	realizar	to fulfill/carry out
comenzar*	to begin/start	ir	to go	recibir	to receive
comprender	to understand	intentar	to try	reconocer	to recognize/admit
conocer	to know (people/places)	jugar*	to play	recordar*	to remember/remind
conseguir*	to get/acquire	leer	to read	resultar	to result/turn out
considerar	to consider	levantar	to lift	saber	to know (information)
contar*	to count/tell story	llamar	to call/name	sacar	to take out
convertir*	to convert	llegar	to arrive	salir**	to leave/go out
correr	to run	llevar	to wear/take/carry	seguir*	to follow/continue
crear	to create	lograr	to achieve	sentir*	to feel
creer	to believe/think	mantener···	to keep/maintain	ser	to be
cubrir	to cover	mirar	to look/watch	servir*	to serve
dar	to give	morir*	to die	suponer**	to suppose
deber	should/to owe	nacer	to be born	tener***	to have
decir***	to say/to tell	necesitar	to need	terminar	to finish/end
dejar	to let/leave	ocurrir	to occur/happen	tocar	to touch/play an instrument/knock
descubrir	to discover	ofrecer	to offer	tomar	to take/drink
dirigir	to direct/manage	oír**	to hear	trabajar	to work
empezar*	to begin/start	pagar	to pay	traer**	to bring/carry
encontrar*	to find	parecer	to seem/look like	tratar	to try/treat
entender*	to understand	partir	to divide/leave	usar	to use
entrar	to enter	pasar	to happen/pass (time)	utilizar	to utilize
escribir	to write	pedir*	to ask for/request	venir***	to come
escuchar	to listen	pensar*	to think	ver	to see
esperar	to wait/hope	perder*	to lose/miss	vestirse*	to dress (oneself)
estar	to be	permitir	to permit/allow	vivir	to live

*stem-changer (pg 67)   **go verb (pg 65)   ***stem-changer & go verb

10

Parts of Speech

Noun

Person, place, or thing

Ex: girl, pencil, teacher, Juan, museum, school

Sentence: I have a **pencil** in my **backpack**.

Adjective

Describes a noun

Ex: blue, bumpy, small, tiny

Sentence: I have a **yellow** pencil in my **tiny** backpack.

Verb

Action or state

Ex: to run, to walk, to eat, to sleep, to leave

Sentence: I **eat** a snack after I **run** home from school.

Adverb

Describes a noun

Ex: quickly, slowly, loudly

Sentence: I work **quickly** and **quietly**.

Pronoun

Replaces a noun

Ex: I, you, him, us, they, it

Sentence: **She** plays with **them** in the park.

Preposition

Linking word

Ex: to, after, at, in

Sentence: I went **to** the party **on** Saturday.

Conjunction

Joins clauses/sentences/words

Ex: and, but, or

Sentence: I want some cookies **and** some milk.

Interjection

Short exclamation

Ex: Ouch! Yikes! Pow!

Sentence: **Ouch!** That hurt!

Direct Object

Answer who? or what? Is receiving the action

Ex: a noun

Sentence: He caught **a ball**.

Indirect Object

Answer to whom? Or to what? Is receiving the action

Ex: a noun

Sentence: I wrote **my mother** a letter.

11

Improve Your Writing Skills

Common Connecting Words and Prepositions	
y	and
o	or
pero	but
porque	because
de	of, from, about
a	to, at
en	in, on, at
por	for, by way of, because of
para	for, to, in order to
con	with
sin	without
sobre	about, on, regarding
hasta	up to, until
entre	between, among
desde	from, since
hacia	toward
contra	against
si	if
sino	but rather
que	that

Expressing Opinion	
Pienso que…	I think that…
Creo que…	I believe that…
En mi opinión...	In my opinion...
A mi modo de ver…	In my view…
Personalmente…	Personally…
Me parece que…	It seems to me that…
Estoy de acuerdo…	I agree…
No estoy de acuerdo...	I don't agree…

Transition Words	
También	Also
Además	Also, In addition, Furthermore
Sin embargo	However
No obstante	Nevertheless
Aunque	Although, Even if
Posiblemente	Possibly
Por ejemplo	For example
Por lo tanto	Therefore
Típicamente	Typically
Desafortunadamente	Unfortunately
Según	According to
Primero	First
Segundo	Second
Tercero	Third
Como resultado	As a result

Time Markers for Sequencing	
Para empezar	To start with
Al principio	In the beginning
Entonces	Then
Después (de)	After, afterwards, next
Más tarde	Later
Inmediatamente	Immediately
Finalmente	Finally
Antes (de)	Before
Primero	First
Mientras	While
Durante	During

12

Referring to Regular Actions in the Present

ahora	now
ahora mismo	right now
hoy	today
hoy en día	nowadays
por la mañana	in the morning
por la tarde	in the afternoon
por la noche	in the evening
todos los días	every day
todas las semanas	every week
todos los meses	every month
una vez a la semana	once a week
cinco veces al mes	five times a month
los lunes	on Mondays
siempre	always
normalmente	normally
a menudo	often
de vez en cuando	from time to time
a veces	sometimes
casi nunca	hardly ever
no…nunca	never
frecuentemente	frequently

Other Time Expressions

el lunes	on Monday
en el invierno	in the winter
en el verano	in the summer
en el otoño	in the fall
en la primavera	in the spring
desde…hasta	from…to…
de…a	from…to…
al principio de	at the beginning of
al final de	at the end of
esta mañana	this morning
esta tarde	this afternoon
esta noche	tonight
esta semana	this week
este mes	this month
este año	this year

Referring to the Past

ayer	yesterday
anteayer	the day before yesterday
ayer por la mañana	yesterday morning
ayer por la tarde	yesterday afternoon
ayer por la noche	yesterday evening
la semana pasada	last week
el mes pasado	last month
el año pasado	last year
el lunes pasado	last Monday
hace una semana	a week ago
hace un mes	a month ago
hace un año	a year ago
antes	before
en 2020	in 2020
de pequeño	as a child
de niño/a	as a child
cuando era niño/a	when I was a child

Referring to the Future

mañana	tomorrow
pasado mañana	the day after tomorrow
mañana por la mañana	tomorrow morning
mañana por la tarde	tomorrow afternoon
mañana por la noche	tomorrow evening
la semana que viene	next week
el mes que viene	next month
el año que viene	next year
el próximo lunes	next Monday
dentro de una semana	in a week's time
dentro de un mes	in a month's time
dentro de un año	in a year's time
en el futuro	in the future
un día	one day
después	afterwards
pronto	soon
más tarde	later

Verbs In Spanish: Learning the Basics

What's a Verb?

A verb is an action. For example, I sleep, he eats, they jump, we dance.

What is an Infinitive Verb?

An infinitive verb is an unconjugated verb. For example: hab**lar** (to speak), com**er** (to eat), o**ír** (to hear). If a verbs ends in –ar, -er, or -ir then it is in the infinitive form. Reflexive verbs in the infinitive form end in –arse, -erse, and -irse. Ex: acost**arse**

The 3 Types of Verbs in Spanish

-ar verbs
-er verbs
-ir verbs

Verb Conjugation

Conjugation means to change the verb from the infinitive form to make it agree with the subject and to say who does the action.

For example: Hablar ⟶ Yo hablo
            (to speak)   (I speak)
                          (I do speak)
                          (I am speaking)

14

What Verb Tense Do I Need?
What are you trying to say?

Referring to the past:

I *had eaten*.	**Pluperfect Tense**	**pg 95**
I *was eating*/I *used to eat*.	**Imperfect Tense**	**pg 60**
I *was eating*.	**Past Progressive**	**pg 92**
I *ate*.	**Preterite Tense**	**pg 61**
If I were to eat…	**Imperfect Subjunctive**	**pg 87**
If I *had been* eating…	**Past Perfect Subjunctive**	**pg 88**
I *would* eat…	**Conditional Tense**	**pg 73**
I *would have* eaten.	**Conditional Perfect Tense**	**pg 97**

Referring to the present:

I *eat*. I *am eating*.	**Present Tense**	**pg 64**
I *am eating*.	**Present Progressive**	**pg 91**
I *have eaten*.	**Present Perfect**	**pg 94**
¡Eat it! ¡Don't eat it!	**Imperative Mood** (Commands)	**pg 75-77**
It's important that *I eat*.	**Present Subjunctive**	**pg 79**

Referring to the future:

I *will eat*.	**Future Tense**	**pg 72**
I *will have eaten*.	**Future Perfect Tense**	**pg 96**

Formulaic Expressions:

I *am going to eat*.	**ir + a + infinitive**	**pg 68**
I *just ate*.	**Acabar + de + infinitive**	**pg 69**
I *have to eat*.	**Tener + que + infinitive**	**pg 70**
If (this) *then* (that) (hypothetical)	**"Si" Clauses**	**pg 89**

Common Classroom Expressions

Common Questions

¿Puedo ir al baño?	May I go to the bathroom?
Tengo sed. ¿Puedo tomar agua?	I'm thirsty. Can I get water?
¿Qué significa...en inglés?	What does...mean in English?
¿Cuál es la fecha de hoy?	What is the date today?
¿Necesitamos tomar apuntes?	Do we need to take notes?
¿Cuál es la tarea?	What's the homework?
¿Me puedes ayudar por favor?	Can you help me please?
¿Puedo ir a la enfermera?	Can I go to the nurse?
¿Cómo se dice…en español?	How do you say…in Spanish?
¿Necesitamos los Chromebooks?	Do we need our Chromebooks?
¿Qué página, por favor?	What page please?
¿Hay preguntas?	Are there any questions?

Other Expressions

Tengo una pregunta	I have a question
No entiendo	I don't understand
Repite por favor	Repeat that please
No sé	I don't know
Más despacio, por favor	Slower please.
La tengo	I have it

Common Prompts

Estoy de acuerdo, porque…	I agree because…
No estoy de acuerdo, porque...	I do not agree because...
En mi opinión…	In my opinion…
Esto me recuerda de…	This reminds me of…
Yo estaba confundido/a cuando…	I was confused when…
No me gustó…	I did not like…
Yo pienso que…	I think that…
Me gusta…	I like...
Descubrí que…	I discovered that…
Mi predicción es que…	I predict that…
¿Me puedes enseñar?	Can you show me…?
¿Por qué piensas eso?	Why do you think that?

Commands/Requests

Escucha(en)	Listen
Repite(an)	Repeat
Lee(an)	Read
Escribe(an)	Write
Contesta(en)	Answer
Levanta(en) la mano	Raise your hand
Saca/saquen	Take out
Abre(an)	Open
Cierra(en)	Close
Vaya a la pizarra	Go to the board
Pregúntele a otro estudiante...	Ask another student....
En parejas	In pairs
Busque un compañero	Look for a partner
Haga la actividad	Do the activity
Formen grupos de	Form groups of...
Déle ____a_____	Give ____to____

Spanish Speaking Countries

North America
Mexico

Europe
Spain

Central America
Guatemala Honduras

Nicaragua Costa Rica Panama El Salvador

Africa
Equatorial Guinea

*Although not the official language, Spanish is widely spoken in: Belize, Barbados, Andorra, US Virgin Islands, Trinidad and Tobago, Netherlands Antilles, and the USA.

South America
Venezuela Ecuador Bolivia Argentina

Uruguay Chile Paraguay Peru Colombia

The Carribean
Dominican Republic Cuba Puerto Rico

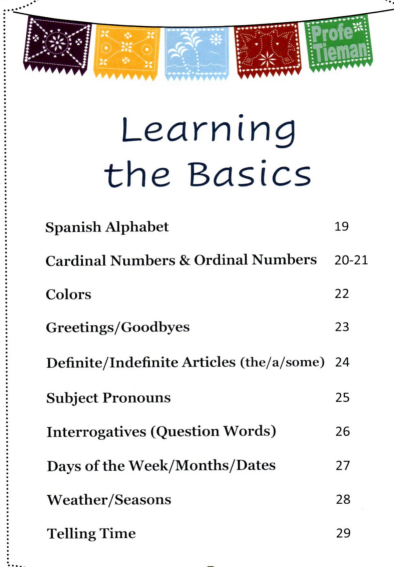

Learning the Basics

The Spanish Alphabet

A	B	C	D	E	F
"ah"	"beh"	"ce"	"deh"	"eh"	"efe"
G	H	I	J	K	L
"heh"	"ah-chay"	"ee"	"hota"	"kah"	"el-ay"
M	N	Ñ	O	P	Q
"Em-ay"	"En-ay"	"En-yay"	"Oh"	"Peh"	"Cu"
R	S	T	U	V	W
"Er-ay"	"Es-ay"	"Teh"	"Ooh"	"Veh"	"Doble-Veh"
X	Y	Z	COMMON SOUNDS		
			CH	LL	RR
"Equis"	"Igiega"	"Zeta"	"Che"	"Ey ay"	"ERR-ay"

Vowels

A	E	I	O	U
"ah"	"eh"	"ee" (WEAK VOWEL)	"Oh"	"Ooh" (WEAK VOWEL)

Los Números

0	cero	18	dieciocho	60	sesenta
1	uno	19	diecinueve	70	setenta
2	dos	20	veinte	80	ochenta
3	tres	21	veintiuno	90	noventa
4	cuatro	22	veintidós	100	cien
5	cinco	23	veintitrés	101	ciento uno
6	seis	24	veinticuatro	200	doscientos
7	siete	25	veinticinco	300	trescientos
8	ocho	26	veintiséis	400	cuatrocientos
9	nueve	27	veintisiete	500	quinientos
10	diez	28	veintiocho	600	seiscientos
11	once	29	veintinueve	700	setecientos
12	doce	30	treinta	800	ochocientos
13	trece	31	treinta y uno	900	novecientos
14	catorce	32	treinta y dos	1,000	mil
15	quince	33	treinta y tres	2,000	dos mil
16	dieciséis	40	cuarenta	1,000,000	millón
17	diecisiete	50	cincuenta	2,000,000	dos millones

Ordinal Numbers

1st (1°, 1ª)*	primero/a, primer
2nd (2°, 2ª)	segundo/a
3rd (3°, 3ª)*	tercero/a,
4th (4°, 4ª)	cuarto/a
5th (5°, 5ª)	quinto/a
6th (6°, 6ª)	sexto/a
7th (7°, 7ª)	séptimo/a
8th (8°, 8ª)	octavo/a
9th (9°, 9ª)	noveno/a
10th (10°, 10ª)	décimo,a
11th (11°, 11ª)	el once
12th (12°, 12ª)	el doce
13th (13°, 13ª)	el trece
14th (14°, 14ª)	el catorce
15th (15°, 15ª)	el quince

1st place: primer* lugar
2nd place: segundo lugar
3rd place: tercer* lugar
4th grade: cuarto grado
5th row: quinta fila
6th floor: sexto piso

*Be sure to drop the "o" for only 1st and 3rd before a singular, masculine noun.

Example:
•primer día
•tercer lugar

The ordinal number agrees in gender and number of the noun it describes.

Example:
•primeros días
•segunda casa

21

LOS COLORES

BLANCO(A/OS/AS) — WHITE

ROJO(A/OS/AS) — RED

ANARANJADO(A/OS/AS) — ORANGE

AMARILLO(A/OS/AS) — YELLOW

VERDE(S) — GREEN

AZUL CELESTE — LIGHT BLUE

AZUL(ES)

AZUL MARINO — DARK BLUE

MORADO(A/OS/AS) — PURPLE

ROSADO(A/OS/AS) — PINK

NEGRO(A/OS/AS) — BLACK

GRIS(ES) (GRAY)   CAFÉ(S)/MORRÓN(ES) (BROWN)

22

Saludos y Despedidas

To Greet Someone...

buenos días	Good morning
buenas tardes	Good afternoon
buenas noches	Good evening/night
¡Hola!	Hello!
¿Cómo te llamas (tú)?	What is your name? (informal)
¿Cómo se llama (Ud.)?	What is your name? (formal)
me llamo...	My name is...
encantado(a)	delighted
igualmente	likewise
mucho gusto	Nice to meet you
señor, Sr.	Sir, Mr.
señora, Sra.	Madam, Mrs.
señorita, Srta.	miss, Ms.
muy bien	very good
así así	so so
tengo sueño	I'm tired
estoy contento/a	I'm happy/content
todo está bien	everything's good
gracias	thank you

To Ask How Someone Is...

¿Cómo estás? (informal)	How are you?
¿Cómo está Ud.? (formal)	How are you?
¿Qué pasa?	What's happening?
¿Qué tal?	How are you?
¿Qué tal tu día?	How was your day?
¿Cómo va?	How's it going?
¿Y tú?/¿Y usted?	And you?

Introductions/Presentations

Te presento a... (informal)	I would like to introduce to you...
Le presento a... (formal)	I would like to introduce to you...
Éste/Ésta es...	This is...
¿De dónde eres? (informal)	Where are you from?
¿De dónde es Ud.? (formal)	Where are you from?

To Say Goodbye...

¡Adiós!	Goodbye
hasta luego	See you later
hasta mañana	See you tomorrow
hasta pronto	See you soon
¡Nos vemos!	See you!
¡Chao!	Bye!
¡Que te vaya bien!	Have a good day!

23

Definite/Indefinite Articles

Definite Articles

There are 4 words for "the" in Spanish

	singular	plural	
	el	los	masculine
	la	las	feminine

*Most nouns that end in "o" are masculine
*Most nouns that end in "a" are feminine
*Definite articles have to agree with the noun in number and gender

Examples:

la mochila —————— las mochilas

el perro ————— los perros

Indefinite Articles

Words that mean "a/an/one/some"

	singular	plural	
	un	unos	masculine
	una	unas	feminine

*Indefinite articles have to agree with the noun in number and gender

Examples:

una mochila ————— unas mochilas

un perro ————— unos perros

24

Spanish Subject Pronouns

	singular	plural
1st person	**YO** I	**NOSOTROS/AS** WE
2nd person	**TÚ** (INFORMAL) YOU	**VOSOTROS/AS*** (INFORMAL) YOU ALL
3rd person	**ÉL** HE **ELLA** SHE	**ELLOS** all males/ males & females THEY/THEM **ELLAS** all females THEY/THEM
2nd person	**USTED**/Ud. (FORMAL) YOU	**USTEDES/Uds.** (FORMAL) YOU ALL

*Vosotros is commonly used in Spain.

1st person: Talking about yourself (I, we)
2nd person: Talking <u>directly</u> to someone/others (you, you all)
3rd person: Talking about someone/others (he, she, they, them)

Examples

1. He eats pizza.   Él come pizza.

2. We go to school.   Nosotros vamos a escuela.

Replacing subjects with subject pronouns:

1. María ⟶ Ella

2. You (informal) ⟶ Tú

3. Juan y yo ⟶ Nosotros

4. Enrique y Carlos ⟶ Ellos

5. Simón y tú ⟶ Vosotros/Uds.

6. You (formal) ⟶ Usted (Ud.)

25

Interrogatives (Question Words)

¿Qué? What?

¿Qué hora es?
What time is it?
¿Qué quieres?
What do you want?

¿Por qué? *Why?*

¿Por qué te gusta la comida italiana?

Why *do you like Italian food?*

¿(De) dónde? (from) where?

¿Dónde estás?
Where *are you?*
¿De dónde eres?
Where *are you from?*
¿Dónde está la tarea?
Where *is the homework?*

¿Cuándo? When*?*

¿Cuándo tienes la clase de español?

When *you do have Spanish class?*

¿Cuál(es)? Which? What?

¿Cuál es la fecha de hoy?
What *is today's date?*
¿Cuáles te gustaron?
Which *ones did you like?*

¿Quién? Who?

¿Quién es tu mejor amigo?
Who is your best friend?

¿Con quién(es)? With whom?

¿Con quiénes jugaban?

Who *were you all playing with?*

¿Adónde? To where?

¿Adónde vas?

(To) where *are you going?*

¿De qué? Of what?

¿De qué material es la pluma?

What *is the pen made of?*

¿Cómo? How? What?

¿Cómo estás?
How *are you?*
¿Cómo te llamas?
What *is your name?*
¿Cómo es Juan?
What *is Juan like?*

¿Cuánto/a/os/as? How much?

¿Cuántos años tienes?
How *old are you?*

La Fecha (The Date)

Los Días de la Semana	
lunes	Monday
martes	Tuesday
miércoles	Wednesday
jueves	Thursday
viernes	Friday
sábado	Saturday
domingo	Sunday

Los Meses del Año	
enero January	**julio** July
febrero February	**agosto** August
marzo March	**septiembre** September
abril April	**octubre** October
mayo May	**noviembre** November
junio June	**diciembre** December

Remember, the Spanish calendar starts on Monday not Sunday and the days and months are <u>NOT</u> capitalized.

In Spanish, the date is written in the following sequence:

(day of the week), el (number) de (month) de (year)

Hoy es <u>lunes,</u> el <u>nueve</u> de <u>septiembre</u> de <u>dos mil veinte.</u>
Today is Monday, September 9th, 2020

For the first day of the month we say "primero" which means "first." Hoy es el **<u>primero</u>** de septiembre.

Use the same format when talking about your birthday:

¿Cuándo es tu cumpleaños?/¿Cuál es la fecha de tu nacimiento?
When is your birthday?

Mi cumpleaños es el nueve de diciembre.
My birthday is December 9th.

¿QUÉ TIEMPO HACE?
(WHAT'S THE WEATHER LIKE?)

hace frío *it's cold*	**hace calor** *it's hot*	**llueve** *it's raining*
hace viento *it's windy*	**hace sol** *it's sunny*	**truena** *it's thundering*
hace fresco *it's brisk*	**está humedad** *it's humid*	**nieva** *it's snowing*
está nublado *it's cloudy*	**hace buen tiempo** *it's good weather*	**hace mal tiempo** *it's bad weather*

LAS ESTACIONES (THE SEASONS)

el invierno	la primavera	el verano	el otoño
winter	*spring*	*summer*	*fall*

Telling Time

¿Qué hora es?   *What time is it?*
Son las/es la*   *It's...*

*We use "es la" for 1 o clock and "son las" for everything else since "es" is for a single hour and "son" is for more than one hour.

Examples:

Son las dos y media de la mañana.   *It's 2:30am.*
Es la *una y cuarto de la tarde.*   *It's 1:15pm.*

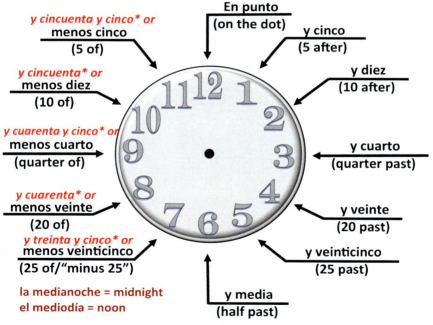

y cincuenta y cinco or
menos cinco
(5 of)

En punto
(on the dot)

y cinco
(5 after)

y cincuenta or
menos diez
(10 of)

y diez
(10 after)

y cuarenta y cinco or
menos cuarto
(quarter of)

y cuarto
(quarter past)

y cuarenta or
menos veinte
(20 of)

y veinte
(20 past)

y treinta y cinco or
menos veinticinco
(25 of/"minus 25")

y veinticinco
(25 past)

la medianoche = midnight
el mediodía = noon

y media
(half past)

It's noon: Es mediodía   **It's midnight: Es medianoche**

de la mañana	in the morning	It's 1:25	Es la una y veinticinco
de la tarde	in the afternoon	It's 5 o'clock	Son las cinco en punto
de la noche	at night	at 5 o'clock	a las cinco en punto

*It is not uncommon for heritage speakers to add versus subtract minutes

Talking About Likes & Dislikes

Gustar & Indirect Object Pronouns

When is it used? ➤ To talk about likes and dislikes.

Indirect Object Pronouns

a mí*	**me**	**nos**	**a nosotros/as***
a ti*	**te**	**os**	**a vosotros/as***
a él/ella/ud.*	**le**	**les**	**a ellos/ellas/uds.***

*used for emphasis/clarification

> Gustar is a <u>backwards verb</u> and means "to be pleasing". This verb does not behave like other verbs where we change the verb to agree with the subject; gustar agrees with what is doing the pleasing. See the examples below.

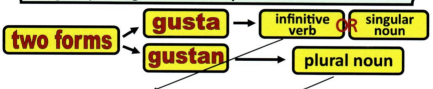

two forms → **gusta** → infinitive verb **OR** singular noun

gustan → plural noun

(A mí) me gusta <u>comer</u> las galletas.

     Eating the cookies is pleasing to me (I like eating cookies).

(A mí) me gustan <u>las galletas</u>.

     Cookies are pleasing to me (I like cookies).

A Profe Tieman *no* le gusta comer las zanahorias.

     Eating carrots is not pleasing to Profe Tieman.

A ella *no* le gustan las zanahorias.

     Carrots are not pleasing to her (She doesn't like carrots).

Other verbs like gustar					
aburrir	to bore	**molestar**	to bother	**parecer**	to seem
doler	to ache/hurt	**encantar**	to love	**importar**	to care/be interested
fascinar	to fascinate	**interesar**	to interest	**quedar**	to fit
faltar	to be lacking/missing			**preocupar**	to worry

¿QUÉ TE GUSTA HACER? ¿POR QUÉ?
(WHAT DO YOU LIKE TO DO? WHY?)

(A mí) me gusta hacer ejercicio <u>porque</u> es divertido.
Exercising is pleasing to me (I like exercise) <u>because</u> it is fun.

¿Y tú? And you?

¿Qué le gusta hacer a tu amigo? ¿Por qué?

What does your friend like to do? Why?

➜**A mi amigo le gusta jugar deportes <u>porque</u> él es muy atlético.**

My friend likes to play sports <u>because</u> he is very athletic.

¿Qué les gusta hacer a Anita y a Carmen? ¿Por qué?

What do Anita and Carmen like to do? Why?

➜ **A Anita y a Carmen (or A ellas) les gusta comer l<u>a</u> pizz<u>a</u> <u>porque</u> <u>es</u> delicios<u>a</u>.**

Anita and Carmen (or they) like to eat pizza <u>because</u> it is delicious.

*Notice that when we say why we like something we use the verb ser for is/are. We use "es" for <u>is</u> and "son" for <u>are</u>. The adjective agrees in gender and number with what we are talking about. If the noun is singular (la pizza) the verb must be singular (es), if the noun is feminine/singular (<u>la</u> pizza) the adjective must be feminine/singular too (delicios<u>a</u>).
Ex: Las papas fritas son deliciosas.

A Pablo le gusta pescar <u>porque</u> es tranquilo.

Pablo likes to fish <u>because</u> it's peaceful.

HOBBIES/LOS PASATIEMPOS

actuar	to act	ir de compras	to go shopping
el atletismo	track and field	ir al parque	go to the park
bailar	to dance	ir a la playa	to go to the beach
el básquetbol	basketball	jugar deportes	to play sports
el béisbol	baseball	jugar juegos de mesa	to play board games
caminar	to walk	jugar videojuegos	to play videogames
cantar	to sing	el lacrosse	lacrosse
cazar	to hunt	leer	to read
cocinar	to cook	los libros	books
comer	to eat	montar a caballo/ en bici/ en moto	to ride a horse/a bike/a motorcycle
conducir/manejar	to drive	montar en monopatín	to ride a scooter/ skateboard
correr	to run	nadar	to swim
decorar	to decorate	nadar en la piscina	to swim in the pool
descansar/relajarse	to rest	las novelas	novels
dibujar	to draw	participar en clubes	to participate in clubs
dormir (o-ue)	to sleep	participar en extracurriculares	to participate in extracurriculars
escribir	to write	pasear al perro	to walk the dog
escuchar	to listen to...	patinar	to skate
escuchar música	to listen to music	pescar	to fish
estar en la naturaleza	to be in nature	pintar	to paint
explorar	to explore	practicar deportes	to play sports
el fútbol	soccer	las revistas	magazines
el fútbol americano	football	sacar fotos	to take photos
la gimnasia	gymnastics	ser voluntario/a	to be a volunteer
hacer ejercicio	to exercise	subir las montañas	to climb mountains
hacer la jardinería	to garden	el tenis	tennis
hacer manualidades	to do arts/crafts	tocar	to touch/play an instrument/knock
hacer la tarea	to do homework	trabajar	to work
hacer videos	to make videos	usar las redes sociales	to use social media
el hockey	hockey	usar la tecnología	to use technology
ir al centro comercial	to go to the mall	ver una película/ un serie	to see a movie/ series
ir al cine	to go to the movies	el vóleibol	volleyball

All About Adjectives
(and some pronouns)

Common Adjectives

aburrido/a	boring	fácil	easy	nuevo/a	new
afortunado/a	lucky	falso/a	false	oscuro/a	dark
agradable	pleasant	feliz	happy	peligroso/a	dangerous
alto/a	tall	feo/a	ugly	pequeño/a	small
amable	friendly	fino/a	thin	pesado/a	heavy
amargo/a	bitter	frío/a	cold	pobre	poor
ancho/a	wide	fuerte	strong	poco/a/os/as	few
apretado/a	tight	generoso/a	generous	preocupado/a	worried
barato/a	cheap	gordo/a	fat	profundo/a	deep
blando/a	soft	grande	large	rápido/a	fast
bonito/a	pretty	grueso/a	thick	relajado/a	relaxed
bueno/a	good	hermoso/a	beautiful	rico/a	rich
caliente	hot	holgado/a	loose/baggy	ruidoso/a	loud
caro/a	expensive	importante	important	seco/a	dry
correcto/a	correct	inteligente	intelligent	seguro/a	safe
corto/a	short length	inútil	useless	sencillo/a	simple
delgado/a	thin/slim	joven	young	sincero/a	sincere
desagadable	unpleasant	largo/a	long	sucio/a	dirty
difícil	difficult	lento/a	slow	superficial	shallow
delicioso/a	delicious	ligero/a	light	tarde	late
divertido/a	fun	limpio/a	clean	temprano	early
dulce	sweet	lleno/a	full	terrible	terrible
duro/a	hard	loco/a	crazy	tímido/a	shy
educado/a	polite	luminoso/a	bright	tranquilo/a	quiet
emocionado/a	excited	mal educado/a	rude	triste	sad
enojado/a	angry	malo/a	bad	útil	useful
estrecho/a	narrow	mojado/a	wet	vacío/a	empty
estúpido/a	stupid	mucho/a/os/as	many/a lot	verdadero/a	true
excelente	excellent	muerto/a	dead	vivo/a	live

Adjective Agreement

In Spanish, an adjective must agree in both *gender* and *number* with the noun it modifies.

MASCULINE SINGULAR	FEMININE SINGULAR	MASCULINE PLURAL	FEMININE PLURAL
serio (serious)	seria	serios	serias
alto (tall)	alta	altos	altas
joven (young)	joven	jóvenes	jóvenes

Él es joven, bajo e inteligente.

Ella es joven, baja y simpática.

Ellos son jóvenes, bajos y simpáticos.

Ellas son inteligentes, delgadas y altas.

Physical Appearance

When talking about yourself:
Soy alto. (*I am tall.*)
When talking about body parts:
Tengo el pelo negro.
(*I have black hair.*)

delgado/a (thin)

gordo/a (fat)

bajo/a (short)

alto/a (tall)

viejo/a (old)

joven (young)

Tener: to have
Yo tengo ojos...

Yo tengo pelo...

marrones (brown) · verdes (green) · azules (blue) · avellanos (hazel) · negros (black)

moreno (dark brown/black)

rubio (blond)

corto (short)

Exception to the rule

Ella <u>es</u> pelirroja.
She is redheaded.

castaño (light brown)

largo (long)

rizado (curly)

gris/canoso (gray)

liso (straight)

Llevar: to wear
Yo llevo...

las gafas del sol (sunglasses)

Los tenis (sneakers)

sombrero (hat)

las gafas (glasses)

Examples

Yo soy alto y joven.	I am tall and young.
Ella tiene ojos verdes.	She has green eyes.
Miguel tiene pelo corto.	Miguel has short hair.
Nosotros llevamos gafas.	We wear glasses.
Soy pelirrojo(a).	I am redheaded.

37

Describing Personality Traits using ser

Yo <u>soy</u> (I am...)

Tú <u>eres</u> (you [informal] are...)

Él/Ella/Usted <u>es</u> (he/she is, you [formal] are...)

Nosotros <u>somos</u> (We are...)

Vosotros <u>sois</u> (You all [informal] are...)

Ellos/Ellas/Ustedes <u>son</u> (they/you all [formal] are...)

vago/a (lazy)

fuerte (strong)
arrogante (arrogant)

travieso/a (unruly)

optimista (optimistic)
extrovertido/a (extroverted)

trabajador/a (hard-working)

Describing Personality Traits					
simpático/a	nice	**aburrido/a**	boring	**sincero/a**	sincere
antipático/a	mean	**alegre/feliz**	happy	**decidido**	determined
seguro/a	confident	**enojado/a**	angry	**introvertido/a**	introverted
inseguro/a	insecure	**irritable**	irritable	**pesimista**	pessimistic
distraído/a	absent-minded	**mentiroso/a**	liar	**paciente**	patient
serio/a	serious	**débil**	weak	**impaciente**	impatient
tonto/a	silly	**abierto/a**	open-minded	**cierto/a**	closed-minded

Abilities & Experiences

Use with Ser: to be (Yo soy...)

adaptable	adaptive	listo/a	intelligent
amable	friendly/nice	meticuloso/a	meticulous
atrevido/a	daring/bold	organizado/a	organized
buen oyente	good listener	positivo/a	positive
cariñoso/a	caring	presentable	presentable
cauteloso/a	cautious	proactivo/a	proactive
colaborativo/a	collaborative	productivo/a	productive
detallista	detail oriented	puntual	punctual
eficiente	efficient	respetuoso/a	respectful
fiable	dependable	responsable	responsible
flexible	flexible	sociable	sociable
honesto/a	honest	trabajador/a	hard-working
licenciado/a	graduate	valiente	brave
persona capaz de resolver problemas		person capable of problem solving	

Use with Tener: to have (Yo tengo...)

un conocimiento informático	computer knowledge	confianza	confidence
una atención de calidad	attention to quality	un buen espíritu	a good spirit
buena administración del tiempo		good time management	
buenas habilidades de comunicación		good communication skills	

Use with Poder: to be able to (Yo puedo...)

aprender rápidamente	to learn quickly	resolver problemas	to solve problems
desarrollar	to develop	seguir instrucciones	to follow instructions
estar en buena forma	to be in good shape	trabajar bien con otras personas	to work well with others
colaborar bien con otros	to collaborate well with others	mantenerse en forma	to stay in shape
mostrar	to show/ demonstrate	hacer buenas decisions	to make good decisions
hablar idiomas con fluidez		to speak languages fluently	

Possessive Adjectives

When are they used? To say things like _my_ car, _your_ house, _his_ shirt, _our_ mother, _their_ brother etc.

MY	OUR
mi/mis	**nuestro/a/os/as**
YOUR (INFORMAL/SINGULAR)	YOUR (INFORMAL/PLURAL)
tu/tus	**vuestro/a/os/as**
HIS/HER/YOUR (FORMAL)	THEIR/YOUR (FORMAL)
su/sus	**su/sus**

NOTE: Possessive adjectives in Spanish agree with the plurality of the noun it describes. A singular noun requires a singular possessive adjective, a plural noun requires a plural possessive adjective <u>no matter</u> if the subject is plural or singular. Nuestro (our) and vuestro (your) are the only adjectives that agree in both gender (masculine/feminine) and number (singular/plural) with the noun that they describe - **NOT** the subject.

Examples		
my car	mi carro	our car nuestr<u>o</u> carr<u>o</u>
her backpack/su mochila		our backpacks nuestr<u>as</u> mochil<u>as</u>
his dog	su perro	his dogs su<u>s</u> perro<u>s</u>
your house tu casa (informal/singular)		your house**s** tu<u>s</u> casa<u>s</u> (informal/<u>singular</u>) **Note: "tus" is plural because "casas" is plural even though the subject (your) is singular**

Possessive Pronouns

To say things like "yours are bigger" or "it's mine." These are different from the adjectives on the previous page because a pronoun does not modify the noun—it takes the place of it.

MINE	**OURS**
mío/a/os/as	**nuestro/a/os/as**
YOURS (INFORMAL/SINGULAR)	**YOURS** (INFORMAL/PLURAL)
tuyo/a/os/as	**vuestro/a/os/as**
HIS/HERS/YOURS (FORMAL)	**THEIRS/YOURS** (FORMAL)
suyo/a/os/as	**suyo/a/os/as**

In Spanish, a possessive pronoun agrees in both *gender* and *number* with the noun it replaces. When the possessive pronoun is used at the beginning of a sentence, typically a definite article (el, la, los, las) is used.

Adjective: Mi casa es roja.   My house is red.

Pronoun: La mía es verde.   Mine is green.

Adjective: Nuestros carros son grandes.   Our cars are big.

Pronoun: Los nuestros son pequeños.   Ours are small.

Adjective: Sus perros son amables.   Her dogs are friendly.

Pronoun: Los tuyos no son amables.   Yours are not friendly.

La mochila roja es suya.   The red backpack is his.

41

Demonstrative Adjectives

"This" and "These" have T's, "That" and "Those" don't!

masculine		feminine	
singular	**plural**	**singular**	**plural**
este this	**estos** these	**esta** this	**estas** these
ese that	**esos** those	**esa** that	**esas** those
aquel that (over there)	**aquellos** those (over there)	**aquella** that (over there)	**aquellas** those (over there)

	(aquí) near me	(allí) farther away	(allá) farthest away
	este libro (this book)	**ese libro** (that book)	**aquel libro** (that book/[over there])
	estos libros (these books)	**esos libros** (those books)	**aquellos libros** (those books/[over there])

Demonstrative Pronouns

masculine		feminine	
singular	**plural**	**singular**	**plural**
éste this[one]	**éstos** these[ones]	**ésta** this[one]	**éstas** these[ones]
ése that[one]	**ésos** those[ones]	**ésa** that[one]	**ésas** those [ones]
aquél that[one] (over there)	**aquéllos** those[ones] (over there)	**aquélla** that[one] (over there)	**aquéllas** those[ones] (over there)

Just add accent marks (only when needed for ambiguity)

So what is the difference between the adjective and the pronoun?
The **adjective** _modifies_ the noun whereas the **pronoun** _takes its place_.

ADJECTIVE	PRONOUN
Yo quiero ese libro. (I want that book.)	**Yo quiero ése.** (I want that one.)

Ser
vs
Estar

SER & ESTAR

Ser and estar are the two most common verbs in the Spanish language and they both mean to be: is/are/was/were etc.. But, how do we know when to use them?   Just follow these helpful tricks...

SER - more permanent*
ESTAR - temporary situations*
*generally speaking

SER

YO **soy**	NOSOTROS/AS **somos**
TÚ **eres**	VOSOTROS/AS **sois**
ÉL ELLA USTED **es**	ELLOS ELLAS USTEDES **son**

ESTAR

YO **estoy**	NOSOTROS/AS **estamos**
TÚ **estás**	VOSOTROS/AS **estáis**
ÉL ELLA USTED **está**	ELLOS ELLAS USTEDES **están**

"How you feel and where you are - always use the verb ESTAR.
What you're like and where you're from - that's when you use the other one."

SER vs. ESTAR	

Yo <u>soy</u> aburrido.
    I am a boring person.
	Yo <u>estoy</u> aburrido.
	    I am (feeling) bored.

<u>Eres</u> bonita.
    You are beautiful (normally).
	¡<u>Estás</u> bonita!
	    You are beautiful (right now).

El café <u>es</u> caliente.
 	
    The coffee is hot (normally).
	¡El café <u>está</u> frío!
	
	    The coffee is cold (it's not normally that way).

SER or ESTAR?

Use the acronyms D.O.C.T.O.R. and P.L.A.C.E. to remember the uses of ser and estar.

SER

Date	**Hoy es el nueve de junio.** Today is June 9th.
Occupation	**Soy profesora.** I am a teacher/professor.
Characteristics	**Ellos son altos y guapos.** They are tall and handsome.
Time	**Son las cinco y media.** It's 5:30.
Origin	**Somos de Madrid.** We are from Madrid.
Relation	**Tú eres mi amigo.** You are my friend.

ESTAR

Position	**La pluma está en mi mochila.** The pen is in my backpack.
Location	**Yo estoy en la escuela.** I am in school.
Action	**Ellos están cantando.** They are singing.
Condition	**Tú estás enfermo.** You are (physically) sick.
Emotion	**Nosotros estamos contentos.** We are happy.

Emociones con Estar

¿Cómo estás?/¿Cómo está (él/ella/Ud.)?
Yo estoy (I am)... / Ella está (she is)...

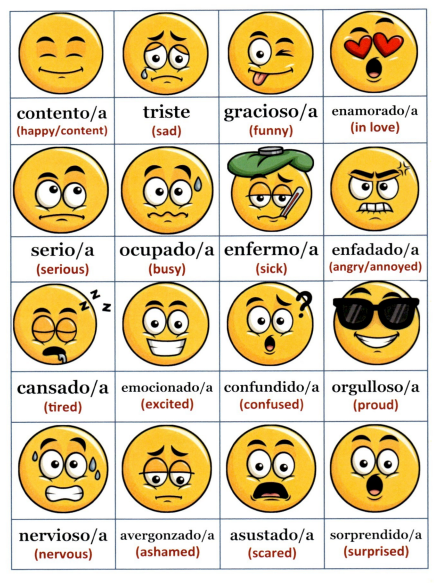

contento/a (happy/content)	**triste** (sad)	**gracioso/a** (funny)	**enamorado/a** (in love)
serio/a (serious)	**ocupado/a** (busy)	**enfermo/a** (sick)	**enfadado/a** (angry/annoyed)
cansado/a (tired)	**emocionado/a** (excited)	**confundido/a** (confused)	**orgulloso/a** (proud)
nervioso/a (nervous)	**avergonzado/a** (ashamed)	**asustado/a** (scared)	**sorprendido/a** (surprised)

Past Participles with Ser/Estar/Nouns

To form –ed endings of words. Ex: tasted/jumped.

When are they used?

A past participle is a verb form <u>not</u> a verb tense and <u>cannot be used on its own</u>. The past participles are used with the verb haber as seen with the perfect tenses (pg 94-97). Ex: I have eaten ("eaten" is the past participle). Past participles can also be used as adjectives when paired with a noun or the verbs ser and estar. Ex: el juguete roto (the broken toy), el juguete está roto ([the state of] the toy is broken).

Forming the Past Participle: See pg 93 for more details

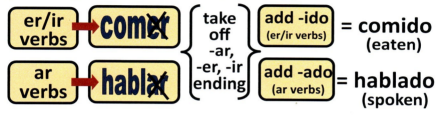

| er/ir verbs | → | com~~er~~ | take off -ar, -er, -ir ending | add -ido (er/ir verbs) | = comido (eaten) |
| ar verbs | → | habl~~ar~~ | | add -ado (ar verbs) | = hablado (spoken) |

When used as an *<u>adjective</u>* after ser/estar or a noun, the past participle changes to agree in <u>gender & number</u>:

Examples:

> La ventana está abierta.
> Las ventanas están abiertas.

Past Participles with Nouns	
la puerta cerrada	the closed door
la ventana abierta	the open window

Past Participles with Ser	
La puerta fue cerrada por Juan.	The door was closed by Juan.
El poema fue escrito por Garcia Lorca.	The poem was written by Garcia Lorca.

Past Participles with Estar	
La puerta está cerrada.	The (state of the) door is closed.
La ventana está abierta.	The (state of the) window is open.

47

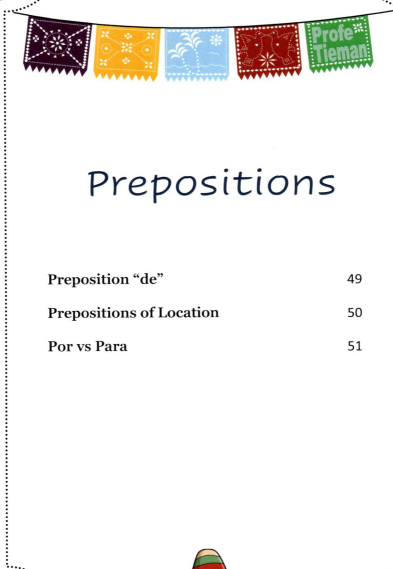

Prepositions

Preposition "de"

de: of, from, about

Preposition "de" has a variety of uses in Spanish.

Origin

Soy **de** Columbia.
   (I am from Columbia.)

Trabajo **de** 9 a 5.
   (I work from 9 to 5.)

Content & Material

Un vaso **de** agua
   (A glass of water)

Una lata **de** aluminio
   (Aluminum can)

Characteristics

La comida era **de** gran calidad.
   (The food was of great quality.)

Possession

We do not use **'s** to show possession in Spanish. Instead, we use "de."

Carlos y Juan's house = La casa **de** Carlos y Juan.
   ("The house of Carlos and Juan.")

Marco's bike = La bicicleta **de** Marco.

Profe Tieman's dog = El perro **de** Profe Tieman.

Location Prepositions con ESTAR

When are they used? ➤ To say where objects/people are located.
Ex: My backpack <u>is on top of</u> the chair.

Follow this easy formula:			
object 1 + estar + preposition + object 2			
1	2	3	4
El lápiz (The pencil)	**está** (is)	**encima de** (on top of)	**la mesa** (the table)

<u>Singular objects</u> use **está "is"**

<u>Plural objects</u> use **están "are"**

For people, conjugate the verb to the subject: yo/estoy, tú/estás, etc.

Nosotros estamos fuera de la escuela.
   We are outside of the school.

Yo estoy dentro del baño.
   I'm in the bathroom.

a + el = al
de + el = del

Prepositions

encima de	on top of	debajo de	underneath
detrás de	behind	delante de	in front of
al lado de	beside	cerca de	close to
lejos de	far from	fuera de	outside of
dentro de	inside of	entre (de)	between
a la izquierda de/ derecha de		on the left/right of	

los libros	el cuaderno
la mochila	la computadora
la silla	la pluma
el celular	el escritorio
el lápiz	el diccionario

PARA es "perfecto"

P urpose
Esta mochila es para mis libros.

E ffect, in order to...
Estudio para sacar buenas notas.

R ecipient
Este regalo es para mi hijo.

F uture/point in time
El proyecto es para viernes.

E mployment
Trabajo para Walmart.

C omparison
Para un caballo viejo, es rápido.

T owards/Destination
Camino para la escuela.

O pinion
Para mí, esta clase es la mejor.

Both can mean "for" but they have other uses/meanings too!

Por or Para?

POR

"Gosh! I Can't Take It For Much Longer!"

G ratitude
Gracias por su ayuda.

I n favor of/on behalf of
Voy a trabajar por Jose porque está enfermo.

C ause/reason
Se me cayó por el piso mojado.

T hrough/along/by
by way of: Viajo por avión.
by; author: El cuento es por Márquez.

I n exchange for
Te doy cinco pesos por la fruta.

F requency
Asisto las clases tres días por semana.

M eans of communicating
Te escribo por correo electrónico.

L ength of time
Trabajé por ocho horas. 51

Other Useful Grammar Concepts

Comparatives/Superlatives

Comparatives of Equality

1. Tan + adjective/adverb + como
   Ex: Isabel es tan inteligente como Margoth.
   (Isabel is as intelligent as Margoth.)
2. Tanto/a/os/as + noun + como
   Ex: Tengo tanta paciencia como tú.
   (I have as much patience as you.)
3. verb + tanto como
   Ex: Yo estudio tanto como tú.
   (I study as much as you.)

Comparatives of Inequality

1. Más or menos + adjective/adverb + que + noun
   Ex: Anita es más baja que Jorge.
   (Anita is shorter than Jorge.)
   Ex: Elena estudia menos que Miguel.
   (Elena studies less than Miguel.)

Comparatives with Numbers

1. Replace que with de before a number:
   Ex: Hay más de veinte libros en el estante.
   (There are more than twenty books on the bookshelf.)

2. If the sentence is negative use que:
   Ex: No hay más que veinte libros en el estante.
   (There are no more than 20 books on the bookshelf.)

Superlatives

1. [Definite Article] + noun + más/menos + adjective + de
   Ex: Roberto es el chico más inteligente de la escuela.
   (Roberto is the most intelligent boy of the school.)

el/la mejor los/las mejores	the best	el/la mayor los/las mayores	the greatest/oldest
el/la peor los/las peores	the worst	el/la menor los/las menores	the least/the youngest

Reflexive Verbs

When are they used? To describe an action that goes back to the recipient of the action (ex: I wash *myself*).

Reflexive Pronouns

me	nos
te	os
se	se

Common reflexive verbs

acostarse (o-ue)	to go to bed
amarse	to love
casarse	to get married
cepillarse los dientes	to brush ones teeth
desmayarse	to faint
despertarse (e-ie)	to wake up
desvestirse (e-i)	to get undressed
dolerse (o-ue)	to hurt oneself
dormirse (o-ue)	to fall asleep
ducharse	to take a shower
enfermarse	to get sick
enojarse	to get angry
hacerse*	to make oneself
irse	to go away/leave
lavarse	to wash oneself
levantarse	to stand/get up
llamarse	to be called
morirse (o-ue)	to die
mirarse	to look at oneself
peinarse	to comb ones hair
ponerse*	to become...
ponerse (ropa)*	to put on (clothes)
preocuparse	to worry
probarse (o-ue)	to try on (clothes)
quedarse	to stay/remain
quitarse (ropa)	to take off (clothes)
sentarse (e-ie)	to seat oneself
sentirse (e-ie)	to feel
verse	to see oneself
vestirse (e-i)	to get dressed

* Go Verbs

Present tense

Me despierto.	I wake (myself) up.
Me siento feliz.	I feel happy.
Me baño.	I bathe myself.
Nos lavamos las manos.	We wash our hands
Ya me voy.	I'm leaving/about to leave.
Me visto.	I get dressed.

Past tense

Me desperté.	I woke (myself) up.
Me cepillé los dientes.	I brushed my teeth.
Me duché.	I showered.
Me vestí.	I got dressed.
Ella se fue tarde.	She left late.
Me enfermé.	I got sick.

se viste

se acuesta

se cepilla los dientes

se baña

Impersonal vs Passive "se"

"Se" has many uses in Spanish. Two of the most common uses are the impersonal and passive "se".

Impersonal "se"

Impersonal "se" is used with the **3rd person singular form (él/ella/ud.)** to express impersonal subjects: one/ you/ people/they.

Examples	
Se puede montar en bicicleta.	**One can** ride a bike.
Se dice que hay muchos problemas en el mundo.	**It is said** that there are a lot of problems in the world.
Se ve el sol en la distancia.	**One sees** the sun in the distance.
Se observa la gente caminando.	**One observes** the people walking.
Se nota la fruta en la pintura.	**One notes** the fruit in the painting.

Passive "se"

Passive "se" behaves in much of the same way as impersonal "se". With Passive "se" the agent of the action is either unknown or simply undefined so the emphasis is placed on the action itself. The conjugated verb is placed in either the **3rd person singular form** (él/ella/ud.) if a <u>singular noun</u> or a <u>verb</u> immediately follows or the **3rd person plural form** (ellos/ellas/uds.) if followed by a <u>plural noun</u>.

Examples	
Se habla español aquí.	Spanish **is spoken** here.
Se permite patina.	Skateboarding **is permitted**.
Se prohibe nadar.	Swimming **is prohibited**.
Se lavan los platos aquí.	Plates **are washed** here.
Se ponen las mochilas aquí.	Backpacks **are placed** here.
Se necesitan permisos.	Permits **needed**.
Se observan las vacas en el prado.	The cows **are observed** in the field.
Se ve el venado herido en la pintura.	The injured deer **is seen** in the painting.
Se revela el secreto en la escena.	The secret **is revealed** in the scene.

Direct/Indirect Object Pronouns

When are they used?

Why use pronouns? Pronouns make communicating more efficient. Without pronouns, if someone asks you, "Did you see Lionel Messi kick that goal?" you would have to say, "Yes, I saw Lionel Messi kick that goal." But, with pronouns, you could say, "Yes, I saw ___him___ kick ___it___."

Direct Object Pronouns

How to find the direct object in a sentence: Just answer **Who?** Or **What?** is receiving the action.

Hint: for direct objects, use the definite article (el (lo), la, los, las)

Direct Object Pronouns

me	nos
te	os
lo/la	los/las

Marco throws the ball.		
Marco	tira	la pelota.
subject	verb	direct object

"Lola is a direct lady."

What does Marco throw?
➡ the ball (direct object)

Replace "la pelota" with a direct object pronoun that matches the noun in <u>gender</u> & <u>number</u> and place it **in front** of the conjugated verb.

Marco <u>la</u> tira. (Marco throws it.)

Indirect Object Pronouns

How to find the indirect object in a sentence: Just answer **To Whom?** Or **To What?** is receiving the action.

Indirect Object Pronouns

me	nos
te	os
le	les

Marco throws María the ball.				
Marco	tira	la pelota	a	María
subject	verb	direct object		indirect object

To whom does he throw?
➡ María

Replace "María" with an indirect object pronoun that matches the subject and plurality of the noun and place it **in front** of the conjugated verb.

Marco <u>le</u> tira la pelota. (Marco throws her the ball.)

Forming Double Object Pronouns

I wrote my mother a letter.					
Yo	(le)	escribí	la carta	a	mi madre.
subj.		verb	direct object		indirect object

Step 1: Replace the direct & indirect object with the appropriate pronoun:

Direct Object Pronouns

me	nos
te	os
lo/la	los/las

la carta → la

Step 2:

mi madre → le

Indirect Object Pronouns

me	nos
te	os
le	les

Rewrite the sentence
with the pronouns in the order
of R.I.D. (reflexive-indirect-direct)
replacing the direct & indirect objects.

I wrote ~~my mother~~ (her) ~~a letter~~ (it).			
Yo	le	la	escribí
subj.	indirect object pronoun	direct object pronoun	verb

But, wait! There's a problem! In Spanish **they don't "le lo" they "se lo."** Whenever there are two pronouns that both begin with an "L" we change the first pronoun to "se."

Step 3: (if applicable)

If you have two pronouns that start with "L" -
change the first pronoun to "se"

Yo se la escribí.
    I wrote it to her.

You can't
le lo, but you
can se lo!

57

Saber vs Conocer

SABER: to know (information/facts/ how to do something)

yo **sé**	nosotros/as **sabemos**
tú **sabes**	vosotros/as **sabéis**
él ella usted **sabe**	ellos ellas ustedes **saben**

Yo no sé.
(I don't know)

Yo sé que 1+1 = 2.

Yo sé bailar.

Ella sabe la respuesta.

I know that 1 + 1 = 2.

I know how to dance.

She knows the answer.

CONOCER: to know of (people/places)

yo **conozco**	nosotros/as **conocemos**
tú **conoces**	vosotros/as **conocéis**
él ella usted **conoce**	ellos ellas ustedes **conocen**

Conocí a tus amigos.
(I met your friends.)

Yo conozco a tu amigo, Mario.

¿Tú conoces a mi hermano?

Ella conoce el español.

Se conocen del colegio.

I know your friend, Mario.

Do you know/have you met my brother?

She knows/speaks Spanish.

They know each other from school.

Indicative Mood
(Past, Present, Future, Conditional)

Used to express actions or ideas that *indicate* something real or concrete such as facts, habitual actions, routines, etc. Exception: The Condition Tense is used for hypothetical situations.

Imperfect (Past) Tense

When is it used? → To talk about events in the past and say things like, "I was dancing" and "I used to dance."

Uses of the Imperfect
"Wasabi Tacos Are Down Right Spicy Ouch!"

Weather	Hacía sol y calor.	It was sunny and hot.
Time	Eran las ocho de la mañana.	It was 8am.
Age	Cuando tenía diez años.	When I was 10 years old.
Descriptions	De niño, era tímido.	As a child, I was shy.
Repeated action	Los martes, preparaba los tacos.	On Tuesdays, I would prepare tacos.
State of being	Ella estaba triste después de ver las noticias anoche.	She was sad after watching the news last night.
Ongoing action	Mi hermano estaba bailando mientras tocaba el piano.	My brother was dancing while I was playing piano.

Imperfect Trigger Words

a veces	sometimes
cada día	everyday
cada año	each year
cada mes	every month
cuando era niño/a	when I was a child
de niño/a	as a child
de vez en cuando	sometimes
los lunes	on Mondays
mientras	meanwhile
muchas veces	many times
nunca	never
siempre	always
todas las semanas	every week
todos los años	every year
todos los días	everyday

-ar verb endings

	yo	nosotros/as
	-aba	**-ábamos**
tú	**-abas**	vosotros/as **-abais**
él ella usted	**-aba**	ellos ellas ustedes **-aban**

-er/ir verb endings

	yo	nosotros/as
	-ía	**-íamos**
tú	**-ías**	vosotros/as **-íais**
él ella usted	**-ía**	ellos ellas ustedes **-ían**

ir: to go

YO	iba	NOSOTROS/AS	íbamos
TÚ	ibas	VOSOTROS/AS	ibais
ÉL ELLA USTED	iba	ELLOS ELLAS USTEDES	iban

ver: to see

YO	veía	NOSOTROS/AS	veíamos
TÚ	veías	VOSOTROS/AS	veíais
ÉL ELLA USTED	veía	ELLOS ELLAS USTEDES	veían

ser: to be

YO	era	NOSOTROS/AS	éramos
TÚ	eras	VOSOTROS/AS	erais
ÉL ELLA USTED	era	ELLOS ELLAS USTEDES	eran

Only 3 irregular verbs!

* Note that the yo form and él/ella/Ud. form are the same in the imperfect.
**There are only 3 irregular verbs & no stem changers in the imperfect.

60

Preterite (Past) Tense

When is it used? ➡ To talk about completed past events and say things like, "I danc**ed**."

Uses of the Preterite "**T**aco **B**ell **I**s **S**crumptious, **S**picy, & **D**elicious!"		
Time period	Hice la tarea por dos horas anoche.	I did homework for 2 hours last night.
Beginning/end	Empecé a lavar los platos.	I started to wash the dishes.
Interrupter	Estaba mirando la televisión cuando llegó mi mamá.	I was watching t.v. when my mom arrived.
Single completed action	Yo fui a la tienda.	I went to the store.
Series of actions	Me desperté, me duché, y me vestí.	I woke up, took a shower, and got dressed.
Definite number of times	Viajé a Costa Rica dos veces.	I traveled to Costa Rica two times.

Preterite Trigger Words	
anoche	last night
anteayer	the day before yesterday
ayer	yesterday
de repente	all of a sudden
dos veces	twice
el año pasado	last year
el mes pasado	last month
entonces	then
hace dos años...	two years ago...
la semana pasada	last week
por fin	finally
tres veces	three times
una vez	once

regular -ar verb endings

yo	-é	nosotros/as	-amos
tú	-aste	vosotros/as	-asteis
él ella usted	-ó	ellos ellas ustedes	-aron

regular -er/-ir verb endings

yo	-í	nosotros/as	-imos
tú	-iste	vosotros/as	-isteis
él ella usted	-ió	ellos ellas ustedes	-ieron

*Note:

Unlike the imperfect tense, the preterite tense has many irregulars (pg 62). ➡

61

Preterite Tense Spelling Changes

car/gar/zar verbs (changes only in the yo form)

car=qué	sacar: to take out		llegar: to arrive		cruzar: to cross	
gar-gué	saqué	sacamos	llegué	llegamos	crucé	cruzamos
zar-cé	sacaste	sacasteis	llegaste	llegasteis	cruzaste	cruzasteis
	sacó	sacaron	llegó	llegaron	cruzó	cruzaron

Y-changers (i changes to y in 3rd person forms)

Some Y-changers like oir, creer, and leer have lots of accents.	leer: to read		oír: to hear		destruir: to destroy	
	leí	leímos	oí	oímos	destruí	destruimos
	leíste	leísteis	oíste	oísteis	destruiste	destruisteis
	leyó	leyeron	oyó	oyeron	destruyó	destruyeron

3rd & 3rd Stem-Changers aka Sandal Verbs

(only -ir verbs that have spelling changes in the present tense will have a spelling change in the preterite but only 'e to i' and 'o to u' and only in the 3rd person sing/pl.

pedir: to ask for		morir: to die		preferer: to prefer		dormir: to sleep	
pedí	pedimos	morí	morimos	preferí	preferimos	dormí	dormimos
pediste	pedisteis	moriste	moristeis	preferiste	preferisteis	dormiste	dormisteis
pidió	pidieron	murió	murieron	prefirió	prefirieron	durmió	durmieron

Irregular Stems

irregular verb endings

yo -e	nosotros/as -imos
tú -iste	vosotros/as -isteis
él ella usted -o	ellos ellas ustedes -ieron/-eron*

*-eron after a "j" stem

Irregular Stems (NO ACCENT MARKS!)

andar	anduv	to walk
conducir	conduj	to drive
decir	dij	to say/tell
estar	estuv	to be
haber	hubo*	there was/were
hacer	hic/hiz	to do/make
poder	pud	to manage
poner	pus	to put/place
querer	quis	to try
saber	sup	to find out (info)
tener	tuv	to have
traer	traj	to bring
venir	vin	to come

ser: to be* / ir: to go*

YO	NOSOTROS/AS
fui	fuimos
TÚ	VOSOTROS/AS
fuiste	fuisteis
ÉL ELLA USTED	ELLOS ELLAS USTEDES
fue	fueron

hacer: to do/make

YO	NOSOTROS/AS
hice	hicimos
TÚ	VOSOTROS/AS
hiciste	hicisteis
ÉL ELLA USTED	ELLOS ELLAS USTEDES
hizo	hicieron

ver: to see

YO	NOSOTROS/AS
vi	vimos
TÚ	VOSOTROS/AS
viste	visteis
ÉL ELLA USTED	ELLOS ELLAS USTEDES
vio	vieron

dar: to give

YO	NOSOTROS/AS
di	dimos
TÚ	VOSOTROS/AS
diste	disteis
ÉL ELLA USTED	ELLOS ELLAS USTEDES
dio	dieron

*ir/ser have the same conjugations in the preterite

Telling a Story in the Past

Verbs that Change Meaning in the Preterite & Imperfect			
Imperfect		**Preterite**	
querer	wanted	querer	tried
no querer	didn't want	no querer	refused
conocer	knew (person)	conocer	met
saber	knew (information)	saber	found out
poder	was/were/used to be able to	poder	managed
tener	had/used to have	tener	received
estar	was/were	estar	became/got

How to Tell a Story in the Past using the Preterite/Imperfect

Use the following as a guide to help you decide which of the two Spanish past tenses is the most appropriate for talking about events in the past.

Imperfect	Preterite
Setting the Scene	**Completed Past Actions**
Where does the story take place?	What happened (completed actions)?
Who was with you?	What was the cause/start of the event?
What lead up to this event?	What was the conclusion?
What were you (or others) doing?	What did you/others do?
Describe the Surroundings	What did you/others hear?
What was the weather like?	Where did you/others go?
What time of year was it?	**Sudden Changes**
How old were you at the time?	Did you or someone get sick all of a sudden?
What time of day was it?	What did you or others try to do?
Describe Yours/Others' Emotions	Did you find out/discover something important?
What were you/others feeling?	**Dialogue**
Talk about what you/others wanted	What did you say/shout/whisper etc.?
Emotional/physical states	What did others say?

Present Tense

When is it used? → To say what is happening right now in the present (I sing, I do sing, I am singing)

-ar verb endings

YO	-o	NOSOTROS/AS	-amos
TÚ	-as	VOSOTROS/AS	-áis
ÉL ELLA USTED	-a	ELLOS ELLAS USTEDES	-an

Hablar
↓
Hablar~~r~~
↓
Yo hablo
(I speak, I do speak, I am speaking)

-er verb endings

Comer (to eat)
↓
Comer~~r~~
↓
Ella come
(She eats, She does eat, She is eating)

YO	-o	NOSOTROS/AS	-emos
TÚ	-es	VOSOTROS/AS	-éis
ÉL ELLA USTED	-e	ELLOS ELLAS USTEDES	-en

-ir verb endings

YO	-o	NOSOTROS/AS	-imos
TÚ	-es	VOSOTROS/AS	-ís
ÉL ELLA USTED	-e	ELLOS ELLAS USTEDES	-en

Vivir (to live)
↓
Vivir~~r~~
↓
Nosotros vivimos
(We live, We do live, We are living)

64

Present Tense Irregulars

 **GO Verbs!** These are verbs that (when conjugated) end in "go" but **only in the yo form**.

TENER: TO HAVE

YO	NOSOTROS/AS
tengo	**tenemos**
TÚ	VOSOTROS/AS
tienes	**tenéis**
ÉL ELLA USTED	ELLOS ELLAS USTEDES
tiene	**tienen**

PONER: TO PUT/PLACE/SET

YO	NOSOTROS/AS
pongo	**ponemos**
TÚ	VOSOTROS/AS
pones	**ponéis**
ÉL ELLA USTED	ELLOS ELLAS USTEDES
pone	**ponen**

DECIR: TO SAY/TELL

YO	NOSOTROS/AS
digo	**decimos**
TÚ	VOSOTROS/AS
dices	**decís**
ÉL ELLA USTED	ELLOS ELLAS USTEDES
dice	**dicen**

HACER: TO DO/MAKE

YO	NOSOTROS/AS
hago	**hacemos**
TÚ	VOSOTROS/AS
haces	**hacéis**
ÉL ELLA USTED	ELLOS ELLAS USTEDES
hace	**hacen**

SALIR: TO LEAVE/GO OUT

YO	NOSOTROS/AS
salgo	**salimos**
TÚ	VOSOTROS/AS
sales	**salís**
ÉL ELLA USTED	ELLOS ELLAS USTEDES
sale	**salen**

OÍR: TO HEAR

YO	NOSOTROS/AS
oigo	**oímos**
TÚ	VOSOTROS/AS
oyes	**oís**
ÉL ELLA USTED	ELLOS ELLAS USTEDES
oye	**oyen**

More GO Verbs

caerse	*(to fall down)*	Me caigo	traer	*(to bring)*	Yo traigo
venir	*(to come)*	Yo vengo	valer	*(to cost/be worth)*	Yo valgo
conseguir	(to get)	Yo consigo	*seguir*	(to follow)	Yo sigo

Present Tense Irregulars Continued

SER: TO BE

YO	soy	NOSOTROS/AS	somos
TÚ	eres	VOSOTROS/AS	sois
ÉL ELLA USTED	es	ELLOS ELLAS USTEDES	son

ESTAR: TO BE

YO	estoy	NOSOTROS/AS	estamos
TÚ	estás	VOSOTROS/AS	estáis
ÉL ELLA USTED	está	ELLOS ELLAS USTEDES	están

IR: TO GO

YO	voy	NOSOTROS/AS	vamos
TÚ	vas	VOSOTROS/AS	vais
ÉL ELLA USTED	va	ELLOS ELLAS USTEDES	van

VER: TO SEE

YO	veo	NOSOTROS/AS	vemos
TÚ	ves	VOSOTROS/AS	veis
ÉL ELLA USTED	ve	ELLOS ELLAS USTEDES	ven

SABER: TO KNOW (INFO)

YO	sé	NOSOTROS/AS	sabemos
TÚ	sabes	VOSOTROS/AS	sabéis
ÉL ELLA USTED	sabe	ELLOS ELLAS USTEDES	saben

OLER: TO SMELL

YO	huelo	NOSOTROS/AS	olemos
TÚ	hueles	VOSOTROS/AS	oléis
ÉL ELLA USTED	huele	ELLOS ELLAS USTEDES	huelen

Irregular Yo Forms

conducir*	Yo conduzco (I drive)	conocer*	Yo conozco (I know people/places)	caber	Yo quepo (I fit[space])
traducir*	Yo traduzco (I translate)	parecer*	Yo parezco (I seem/look like)	dar	Yo doy (I give)
aparecer*	Yo aparezco (I appear)	ofrecer*	Yo ofrezco (I offer)	saber	Yo sé I know

*Most verbs that end in cer/cir, the "c " changes to "cz" in the yo form.

Common Stem Changing Verbs

aka "boot/shoe" verbs

A stem changing verb is a verb with a spelling change in the stem of the verb to make it sound better. The stem is the part of the verb that comes before its –ar, -er, -ir ending. For example: "mov" is the stem of movar

O ➡ UE		E ➡ IE		E ➡ I	
acordar	to remember	acertar	to be right	competir	to compete
acostarse	to go to bed	advertir	to warn	conseguir	to achieve
almorzar	to eat lunch	calentar	to heat/warm up	corregir	to correct
aprobar	to pass/approve	cerrar	to close	despedirse	to fire/say goodbye
contar	to count/to tell	confesar	to confess	elegir	to choose
costar	to cost	consentir	to consent	freír	to fry
demostrar	to demonstrate	convertir	to convert/change	impedir	to impede/avoid
dormir	to sleep	comenzar	to start/begin	maldecir	to curse
devolver	to return	defender	to defend	medir	to measure
encontrar	to find	divertirse	to have fun	pedir	to ask for
envolver	to wrap/cover	encender	to light/switch on	reír	to laugh
morder	to bite	empezar	to start/begin	repetir	To repeat
morir	to die	fregar	to mop	seguir	to continue/follow
mostrar	to show	hervir	to boil	servir	to serve
movar	to move	negar	to deny	vestirse	to dress oneself
poder	to be able to	mentir	to lie	I ➡ IE	
probar	to prove/to try	pensar (en)	to think (about)	adquirir	to acquire
recordar	to remember	perder	to lose	inquirir	to inquire into
resolver	to resolve	preferir	to prefer	U ➡ UE	
sonar	to sound	querer	to want	jugar	to play
soñar (con)	to dream (about)	recomendar	to recommend		
tostar	to toast/suntan	sentir	to feel		
volar	to fly	sugerir	to suggest		
volver	to come back	temblar	to tremble/shake		

yo Juego	nosotros/as Jugamos
tú Juegas	vosotros/as Jugáis
él ella usted Juega	ellos ellas ustedes Juegan

But WAIT! There are NO spelling changes in the nosotros/vosotros forms!

ir + a + infinitive

When is it used? To say what you or others are going to do in the near future.
Ex: "I am going to travel to Spain."

YO **voy**	NOSOTROS/AS **vamos**
TÚ **vas**	VOSOTROS/AS **vais**
ÉL ELLA USTED **va**	ELLOS ELLAS USTEDES **van**

Use "ir + a" to talk about the events the future without having to use the future tense!

Examples:

- Mañana, Manuel <u>va a nadar</u> en la piscina.
  Tomorrow, Manuel <u>is going to swim</u> in the pool.

- Yo <u>voy a jugar</u> al tenis con mis amigos.
  <u>I am going to play</u> tennis with my friends.

- Nosotros <u>vamos al cine</u> este fin de semana.
  <u>We are going to the movies</u> this weekend.

- Yo <u>voy a la tienda</u> para comprar comida.
  <u>I am going to the store</u> to buy food.

- Ellos <u>van a ganar</u> el partido el viernes.
  <u>They are going to win</u> the game on Friday.

Acabar + de + infinitive

When is it used? To say what has just happened.
Ex: *"I just ate."*

YO **acabo**	NOSOTROS/AS **acabamos**
TÚ **acabas**	VOSOTROS/AS **acabáis**
ÉL ELLA USTED **acaba**	ELLOS ELLAS USTEDES **acaban**

Use "acabar" to talk about the immediate past without even having to use the past tense!

- Profe Tieman <u>acaba de leer</u> un libro.
  Profe Tieman <u>just read</u> a book.

- Yo <u>acabo de terminar</u> con mi tarea.
  I <u>just finished</u> with my homework.

¡Ellos <u>acaban de ganar</u> el partido!
They <u>just won</u> the game!

No tengo hambre porque yo <u>acabo de comer</u>.
I am not hungry because I <u>just ate</u>.

Los acabo de comprar.
OR Acabo de comprarlos
I just bought them (the jeans).

Stick it to it rule!
Direct/Indirect object pronouns can be placed on the ends of:
Infinitives
Gerunds (ando/iendo)
Commands

El verbo tener: to have

YO	NOSOTROS/AS
tengo	**tenemos**
TÚ	VOSOTROS/AS
tienes	**tenéis**
ÉL ELLA USTED **tiene**	ELLOS ELLAS USTEDES **tienen**

Tener has an e-ie spelling change in the stem in all forms except for the yo, nosotros and vosotros forms. Tener is also a "go" verb: the verb ends in "go" but only in the "yo" form.

Examples:

(Yo) tengo un gato. *I have a cat.*

Tenemos mucha tarea. We have a lot of homework.

tener has other uses and meanings

tener + que + infinitive = to have to
(Unconjugated verb) **do something**

(Yo) tengo que hacer mi tarea.

I have to do my homework.

Miguel y Juan tienen que ir a escuela.

Miguel and Juan have to go to school.

¿A qué hora tienes que acostarte?

What time do you have to go to bed?

Tener Expressions

Tener sueño (to be tired)	**Tener dolor (de)** (to have pain (of)/to hurt)	**Tener hambre** (to be hungry)
Tener sed (to be thirsty)	**Tener calor** (to be hot [temperature])	**Tener frío** (to be cold)
Tener miedo (to be afraid)	**Tener suerte** (to be lucky)	**Tener prisa** (to be in a hurry)

tener razón	to be right, correct	no tener razón	to be wrong
tener # años	to be # years old	tener celos	to be jealous
tener lugar	to take place	tener cuidado	to be careful
tener en cuenta	to take into account, to consider…	tener ganas de…	to feel like…

Examples:

(Yo) tengo ganas de comer. —————— I feel like eating.

Anita tiene razón. ————————— Anita is right/correct.

Carlos y Ricardo tienen frío. —— Carlos and Ricardo are cold.

¿Tienes sueño? ————————————— Are you tired?

Future Tense

When is it used? ➤ To say things that will happen in the future like "*I will be rich and famous*."

-ar/er/ir verb endings

We don't <u>drop</u> the –ar/-er/-ir in the future!

YO -é	**NOSOTROS/AS** -emos
TÚ -ás	**VOSOTROS/AS** -éis
ÉL ELLA USTED -á	**ELLOS ELLAS USTEDES** -án

Forming the Future Tense:

comer + endings

yo comeré
(I will eat)

Ejemplos:

Yo bailaré ———————————————— I will dance.

Tú aprenderás. ———————————— You will learn.

Nosotros iremos de compras. ———— We will go shopping.

Irregular Future Tense Verb Stems*

decir	*to say/tell*	dir-
haber	*there will be*	habrá (1 form)
hacer	*to do/make*	har-
poder	*to be able to*	podr-
poner	*to put/place/set*	pondr-
querer	*to want*	querr-
saber	*to know (info)*	sabr-
salir	*to leave*	saldr-
tener	*to have*	tendr-
valer	*to be worth*	valdr-
venir	*to come*	vendr-

Tú serás rico y famoso y vivirás en España.

*Verbs that contain these stems will also have a spelling change. Ex: man**tener**, su**poner**.

72

The Conditional Tense
aka "The Diarrhea Verb Tense"

IF YOU HAVE DIARRHEA THEN YOU HAVE A CONDITION...
ALL VERBS END IN SOME FORM OF –RÍA IN THE CONDITIONAL.

 When is it used?

To talk about what you or others *would do*.
Ex: *"I would buy a house if I had the money."*

ar/er/ir verb endings

YO	**-ía**	NOSOTROS/AS	**-íamos**
TÚ	**-ías**	VOSOTROS/AS	**-íais**
ÉL ELLA USTED	**-ía**	ELLOS ELLAS USTEDES	**-ían**

Forming the Conditional Tense:

Start with the infinitive verb + **ADD the conditional endings**

We **DON'T** drop the –ar/-er/-ir in the conditional!

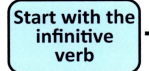 **llorar** ⟶ **(Yo) lloraría**
(to cry) (I would cry)

conditional tense irregulars

decir	*to say/tell*	dir-	saber	*to know (info)*	sabr-
haber	*there will be*	habría (1 form)	salir	*to leave*	saldr-
hacer	*to do/make*	har-	tener	*to have*	tendr-
poder	*to be able to*	podr-	valer	*to be worth*	valdr-
poner	*to put/place*	pondr-	venir	*to come*	vendr-
querer	*to want*	querr-	*Same irregulars as the future tense		

Imperative Mood

(Commands)

Used to express demands and give orders.

Informal Commands
(Imperative Mood)

Affirmative Commands

How to form affirmative commands:

Conjugate the verb to the 3rd person singular (él/ella/usted form of the *PRESENT TENSE*).

Hablar (to talk/speak) ➡ **¡Habla!** (Speak!)

Comer (to eat) ➡ **¡Come!** (Eat!)

When using pronouns:

Attach the pronoun(s) to the end of the command, then add an accent mark on the third syllable from the end (fourth syllable when using two pronouns). If the command has only one pronoun and only consists of two syllables, an accent mark is not required. Ex: Hazlo.
Pronouns: me, te, le, nos, os, les, se, lo, la, los, las

Examples:

Divertirse (to have fun) = **¡Diviértete!**

Ducharse (to take a shower) = **¡Dúchate!**

¡Cómelo! (Eat it) **¡Tómalo!** (Drink it!)

¡Hazlo! (Do it!) **¡Dímelo!** (Tell it to me!)

irregulars		
venir	Ven	V i n
decir	Di	D i e s e l
salir	Sal	
hacer	Haz	h a s
tener	Ten	t e n
ir	Ve	
poner	Pon	w e a p o n s
ser	Sé	

Vin Diesel has ten weapons

Negative Commands

yo form of verb (present tense) **– o +** **es** (ar verbs) **as** (er/ir verbs)

Hablar (to talk/speak) ➡ **¡No hables!** (Don't speak!)

Comer (to eat) ➡ **¡No comas!** (Don't eat!)

Tomar (to take/drink) ➡ **¡No tomes!** (Don't drink!)

When using pronouns:

Place the pronoun before the negative command.

Pronouns: me, te, le, nos, os, les, se, lo, la, los, las

Examples:

Divertirse (to have fun) = **¡No te diviertas!**

Ducharse (to take a shower) = **¡No te duches!**

irregulars "SIDE"	
ser	no seas
ir	no vayas
dar	no des
estar	no estés
–car verbs tocar	-ques no toques
-gar verbs llegar	-gues no llegues
-zar verbs abrazar	-ces no abraces

Spelling changes in the yo form of the present tense occur with negative tú commands

Formal Commands
(Imperative Mood)

(No) **yo form of verb** *(present tense)* **– O +** **e(n)** (ar verbs) / **a(n)** (er/ir verbs)

↑ Just add "no" here for negative commands

↑ **Usted** (singular)

↖ **Ustedes** (plural)

Hablar	➡	¡Hable(n)/No hable(n)!
		(Speak/Don't speak!)
Comer	➡	¡Coma(n)/No coma(n)!
		(Eat/Don't eat!)
Tener	➡	¡Tenga(n)/No tenga(n)!
		(Take/Don't take!)

When using pronouns:

For affirmative commands, attach the pronoun to the end of the command then add an accent mark on the third syllable from the end (or the fourth syllable for two pronouns). For negative commands, place the pronoun(s) in front. When using multiple pronouns, follow the order of R.I.D. (reflexive-indirect-direct). Examples:

dormirse (to go to sleep)

➡ **duérmase** (go to sleep)

➡ **no se duerma** (Don't go to sleep)

decir (to say/tell)

➡ **dígannoslo** (Tell it to us)

➡ **no nos lo digan** (Don't tell it to us)

irregulars

infinitive	singular	plural
dar	dé	den
estar	esté	estén
ir	vaya	vayan
ser	sea	sean
–car verbs tocar	-que toque	-quen toquen
-gar verbs llegar	-gue llegue	-guen lleguen
-zar verbs abrazar	-ce abrace	-cen abracen

Spelling changes in the yo form of the present tense occur with formal commands.

Reflexive Pronouns

me	nos
te	os
se	se

Indirect Object Pronouns

me	nos
te	os
le	les

Direct Object Pronouns

me	nos
te	os
lo/la	los/las

Nosotros Commands
(aka the Dora the Explorer verb tense: ¡Vámonos!)

(No) yo form of verb (present tense) **– O + emos** (ar verbs) **amos** (er/ir verbs)

Hablar	➡	¡(No) hablemos!	Let's (not) talk!
Comer	➡	¡(No) comamos!	Let's (not) eat!
Bailar	➡	¡(No) bailemos!	Let's (not) dance!

When using pronouns:

For affirmative commands, attach the pronoun(s) to the end of the command then add an accent mark on the third syllable from the end. For negative commands, place the pronoun(s) in front. When using multiple pronouns, follow the order of R.I.D. (reflexive-indirect/direct). Examples:

Affirmative Commands w/ Pronouns

Verb: Levantarse: to get up
Step 1. Conjugate: Levantemos
Step 2. Drop the "S"
Step 3. Change "se" to "nos"
Step 4. Put it together and add the accent mark on third syllable from the end: **Levantémonos**

Negative Commands w/ Reflexive Verbs

Verb: Levantarse: to get up
Step 1. Conjugate: Levantemos
Step 2. Change "se" to "nos"
Step 3. Add a no
Step 4. Put it together

No nos levantemos

irregulars	
dar	demos
estar	estemos
ir	vamos (no vayamos)
saber	sepamos
ser	seamos
ver	veamos
–car verbs tocar	-quemos toquemos
-gar verbs llegar	-guemos lleguemos
-zar verbs abrazar	-cemos abracemos

Spelling changes in the yo form of the present tense occur with nosotros commands.

Reflexive Pronouns		Indirect Object Pronouns		Direct Object Pronouns	
X	nos	me	nos	me	nos
X	X	te	os	te	os
X	X	le	les	lo/la	los/las

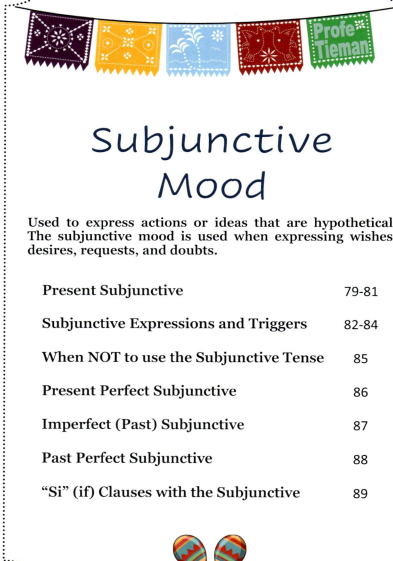

Subjunctive Mood

Used to express actions or ideas that are hypothetical. The subjunctive mood is used when expressing wishes, desires, requests, and doubts.

Present Subjunctive

To talk about hypothetical/uncertain situations, wishes, doubts, emotions, requests, suggestions etc. Ex: *"I hope that my kids clean their rooms,"* "I suggest that you study for your Spanish test" etc.

Used with: Present Tense
Future Tense
Commands

-ar verb endings

YO -e	NOSOTROS/AS -emos
TÚ -es	VOSOTROS/AS -éis
ÉL ELLA USTED -e	ELLOS ELLAS USTEDES -en

-er/-ir verb endings

YO -a	NOSOTROS/AS -amos
TÚ -as	VOSOTROS/AS -áis
ÉL ELLA USTED -a	ELLOS ELLAS USTEDES -an

Forming the Subjunctive Mood:

-ar verbs take -er endings & -er/-ir verbs take -ar endings.

limpiar
(to clean) → limpio
put in the *yo form* of the present tense → -O
take off the "O" + subjunctive endings

→ = ellos limpien
(they clean)

Examples:

These examples begin in the present tense and then trigger the use of the present subjunctive after "que."

Yo quiero que mis niños limpien sus cuartos.
I want that my kids clean their rooms.

Mis maestros sugieren que yo complete mi tarea.
My teachers suggest that I complete my homework.

Yo espero que tú comas almuerzo conmigo en la cafetería hoy.
I hope that you eat lunch with me in the cafeteria today.

Present Subjunctive Irregulars

car/gar/zar verbs

sacar: to take out

YO	NOSOTROS/AS
saque	saquemos
TÚ	VOSOTROS/AS
saques	saquéis
ÉL ELLA USTED saque	ELLOS ELLAS USTEDES saquen

llegar: to arrive

YO	NOSOTROS/AS
llegue	lleguemos
TÚ	VOSOTROS/AS
llegues	lleguéis
ÉL ELLA USTED llegue	ELLOS ELLAS USTEDES lleguen

empezar: to begin

YO	NOSOTROS/AS
empiece	empecemos
TÚ	VOSOTROS/AS
empieces	empecéis
ÉL ELLA USTED empiece	ELLOS ELLAS USTEDES empiecen

car → que   **gar → gue**   **zar → ce**

Irregular yo forms

conocer: to know

YO	NOSOTROS/AS
conozca	conozcamos
TÚ	VOSOTROS/AS
conozcas	conozcáis
ÉL ELLA USTED conozca	ELLOS ELLAS USTEDES conozcan

conducir: to drive

YO	NOSOTROS/AS
conduzca	conduzcamos
TÚ	VOSOTROS/AS
conduzcas	conduzcáis
ÉL ELLA USTED conduzca	ELLOS ELLAS USTEDES conduzcan

parecer: to seem

YO	NOSOTROS/AS
parezca	parezcamos
TÚ	VOSOTROS/AS
perezcas	parezcáis
ÉL ELLA USTED perezca	ELLOS ELLAS USTEDES perezcan

ver: to see

YO	NOSOTROS/AS
vea	veamos
TÚ	VOSOTROS/AS
veas	veáis
ÉL ELLA USTED vea	ELLOS ELLAS USTEDES vean

GO Verbs in the present subjunctive

*oír   *traer
*venir *salir
*valer

poner: to put

YO	NOSOTROS/AS
ponga	pongamos
TÚ	VOSOTROS/AS
pongas	pongáis
ÉL ELLA USTED ponga	ELLOS ELLAS USTEDES pongan

seguir: to follow/continue

YO	NOSOTROS/AS
siga	sigamos
TÚ	VOSOTROS/AS
sigas	sigáis
ÉL ELLA USTED siga	ELLOS ELLAS USTEDES sigan

decir: to say/tell

YO	NOSOTROS/AS
diga	digamos
TÚ	VOSOTROS/AS
digas	digáis
ÉL ELLA USTED diga	ELLOS ELLAS USTEDES digan

tener: to have

YO	NOSOTROS/AS
tenga	tengamos
TÚ	VOSOTROS/AS
tengas	tengáis
ÉL ELLA USTED tenga	ELLOS ELLAS USTEDES tengan

hacer: to do/make

YO	NOSOTROS/AS
haga	hagamos
TÚ	VOSOTROS/AS
hagas	hagáis
ÉL ELLA USTED haga	ELLOS ELLAS USTEDES hagan

caer: to fall

YO	NOSOTROS/AS
caiga	caigamos
TÚ	VOSOTROS/AS
caigas	caigáis
ÉL ELLA USTED caiga	ELLOS ELLAS USTEDES caigan

Present Subjunctive Irregulars Cont.

-ar/-er stem changing verbs

-ar/-er verbs **DO NOT** have spelling changes in the nosotros/vosotros forms

pensar (e-ie)= to think

YO		NOSOTROS/AS	
piense		pensemos	
TÚ		**VOSOTROS/AS**	
pienses		penséis	
ÉL ELLA USTED	piense	**ELLOS ELLAS USTEDES**	piensen

poder (o-ue)= to be able to

YO		NOSOTROS/AS	
pueda		podamos	
TÚ		**VOSOTROS/AS**	
puedas		podáis	
ÉL ELLA USTED	pueda	**ELLOS ELLAS USTEDES**	puedan

-ir stem changing verbs

-ir verbs **DO** have spelling changes in the nosotros/vosotros forms but <u>only e-i and o-u.</u>

pedir (e-i)= to think

YO	NOSOTROS/AS
pida	pidamos
TÚ	**VOSOTROS/AS**
pidas	pidáis
ÉL ELLA USTED pida	**ELLOS ELLAS USTEDES** pidan

divertirse (e-ie)= to have fun

YO	NOSOTROS/AS
me divierta	nos divirtamos
TÚ	**VOSOTROS/AS**
te diviertas	os divirtáis
ÉL ELLA USTED se divierta	**ELLOS ELLAS USTEDES** se diviertan

morir (o-ue)= to die

YO	NOSOTROS/AS
muera	muramos
TÚ	**VOSOTROS/AS**
mueras	muráis
ÉL ELLA USTED muera	**ELLOS ELLAS USTEDES** mueran

servir (e-i)= to serve

YO	NOSOTROS/AS
sirva	sirvamos
TÚ	**VOSOTROS/AS**
sirvas	sirváis
ÉL ELLA USTED sirva	**ELLOS ELLAS USTEDES** sirvan

sentirse (e-ie)= to feel

YO	NOSOTROS/AS
me sienta	nos sintamos
TÚ	**VOSOTROS/AS**
te sientas	os sintáis
ÉL ELLA USTED se sienta	**ELLOS ELLAS USTEDES** se sientan

dormir (o-ue)= to sleep

YO	NOSOTROS/AS
duerma	durmamos
TÚ	**VOSOTROS/AS**
duermas	durmáis
ÉL ELLA USTED duerma	**ELLOS ELLAS USTEDES** duerman

Irregulars: "DISHES"

dar = to give

YO	NOSOTROS/AS
dé	demos
TÚ	**VOSOTROS/AS**
des	deis
ÉL ELLA USTED dé	**ELLOS ELLAS USTEDES** den

ir = to go

YO	NOSOTROS/AS
vaya	vayamos
TÚ	**VOSOTROS/AS**
vayas	vayáis
ÉL ELLA USTED vaya	**ELLOS ELLAS USTEDES** vayan

ser = to be

YO	NOSOTROS/AS
sea	seamos
TÚ	**VOSOTROS/AS**
seas	seáis
ÉL ELLA USTED sea	**ELLOS ELLAS USTEDES** sean

estar = to be

YO	NOSOTROS/AS
esté	estemos
TÚ	**VOSOTROS/AS**
estés	estéis
ÉL ELLA USTED esté	**ELLOS ELLAS USTEDES** estén

saber = to know

YO	NOSOTROS/AS
sepa	sepamos
TÚ	**VOSOTROS/AS**
sepas	sepáis
ÉL ELLA USTED sepa	**ELLOS ELLAS USTEDES** sepan

*haber has only one form
"haya"
("there will be")

Subjunctive Triggers

HOW and **WHEN** to use the subjunctive:
Remember, subjunctive is a **"WEIRDO"**

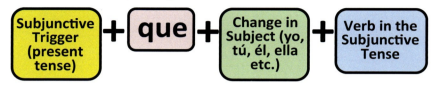

W	**ISHES**
	Quiero que tú hagas la tarea.
	I want that you do the homework.

E	**MOTIONS**
	Me sorprende que el libro sea interesante.
	I am surprised that the book is interesting.

I	**MPERSONAL PHRASES**
	(that express doubts/wishes/emotions etc.)
	¡Es imposible que ella coma tanto!
	It's impossible that she eats that much!

R	**EQUESTS**
	Te recomendamos que no fumes más.
	We recommend that you not smoke anymore.

D	**OUBTS**
	Yo dudo que tu novia sea guapa.
	I doubt that your girlfriend is pretty.

O	**JALÁ**
	Ojalá (que) Profe Tieman no nos dé mucha tarea.
	"I hope/God willing" Profe Tieman doesn't give us much homework.

Subjunctive Trigger Words/Phrases

Wishes/Emotions

desear	to desire
esperar	to hope
insistir en	to insist
Me alegra que	I am happy that
Me enfada que	I'm annoyed that
necesitar	to need
ojalá	I hope that/God willing
permitir	to allow/permit
preferir (e-ie)	to prefer
prohibir	to prohibit
querer (e-ie)	to want
sentir(se) (e-ie,i)	to be sorry that
sorprenderse	to be surprised
temer(se)	to fear that
tener (e-ie) miedo de	to be afraid that

Requests/Doubts

recomendar (e-ie)	to recommend
sugerir (e-ie)	to suggest
dudar	to doubt
negar (e-ie)	to deny
no creer	to not believe
no estar seguro/a (de)	to not be sure of
no es cierto*	it's not certain
no es verdad*	it's not true
es imposible*	it's impossible
es improbable*	it's improbable
(no) es posible*	it's (not) possible
(no) es probable*	it's (not) probable
quizás/tal vez	maybe/perhaps

Impersonal Phrases*
(that express uncertainly/doubts/wishes/emotions)

es bueno que	it's good that
es importante que	it's important that
es lógico que	it's logical that
es malo que	it's bad that
es mejor que	it's better that
es necesario que	it's necessary that
es peligroso que	it's dangerous that
es raro que	it's rare/strange that
es ridículo que	it's ridiculous that
es triste que	it's sad that
es una lástima que	it's a pity that
es sorprendente que	it's surprising that
es justo/injusto que	it's fair/unfair that

WISHES/EMOTIONS
Yo espero que tú **estudies**.
I hope that you study.

REQUESTS
Te sugiero que tú **escuches**.
I suggest that you listen.

DOUBTS
Yo dudo que tú **saques** buenas notas.
I doubt that **you get** good grades.

NOTE...
Not all impersonal expressions require the subjunctive (see pg 85).

IMPERSONAL PHRASES IN THE SUBJUNCTIVE
Es importante que tú **estudies**.   **It's important that you study.**
Es malo que no **limpies** tu cuarto.   **It's bad that you don't clean your room.**

¡OJALÁ!
Ojalá (que) **me llame**.   **Hopefully (God willing), he calls me.**

Subjunctive Triggers Cont.

You can't escape ESCAPA!

There are conjunctions that always require the subjunctive.
But the "que" must be present
(not to be confused with prepositions).

En caso de que	(in case)	Lleva una chaqueta en caso de que llueva.
Sin que	(without)	No sé como explicar sin que mi madre sepa la verdad.
Con tal de que	(provided that)	Voy al cine con mi hermano con tal de que él tenga el dinero.
Antes de que	(before)	¡No me digas cómo termina la película antes de que yo la vea!
Para que	(so that)	Yo estudio para que mis padres estén contentos.
A menos que	(unless)	No saldré con él a menos que se peine el pelo.

Conjunctions that require the subjunctive when talking about future events that are uncertain: "MATCHED"

Mientras	(as long as)	Yo haré la tarea mientras (que) me ayudes.
Aunque	(although/even if)	Aunque entremos la tienda, no voy a encontrar lo que busco.
Tan pronto como	(as soon as)	Comeremos tan pronto como nuestro amigo llegue.
Cuando	(when)	No puedo estudiar cuando me mires.
Hasta que	(until)	Vamos a quedarnos aquí hasta que ella haya ido.
En cuanto	(as soon as)	Veremos la película en cuanto llegue la pizza.
Después de que	(after)	Nos acostaremos después de que termine el partido.

When NOT to use the Subjunctive

When expressing a wish, desire, request, or suggestion using verbs like querer, desear, and esperar in the subjunctive, a **change is subject is necessary**. If there is no change in subject, the infinitive verb is used because of the rule: *when two verbs go walking only the first one does the talking*. See the examples below:

 Not Subjunctive

 Subjunctive

Only one subject: use the <u>infinitive</u> (not the subjunctive)

 I want to read a book → Yo quiero **<u>leer</u>** un libro.

Expressing a wish/desire with TWO subjects: use the subjunctive

 I want you to read a book → Yo quiero que **tú leas** un libro.

INDICATIVE/INFINITVE VS	SUBJUNCTIVE
Estudio <u>antes de</u> **cenar**.	Estudio ***<u>antes de que</u>*** mi madre *prepare la cena*.
Estudio español <u>para</u> **hablar** con mi abuela.	Estudio español *<u>para que</u>* mi abuela <u>esté</u> contenta.

Not ALL impersonal phrases require the subjunctive:

* **<u>Don't</u>** use the subjunctive with impersonal phrases that denote ***certainty*** **(creer/pensar/es cierto que/es obvio que/ es verdad que/estar seguro que)**

Don't use the subjunctive when discussing people or things that are known to exist:

 Busco a alguien que *habla* español. (not subjunctive)

 Busco a alguien que hable español. (w/ subjunctive means you don't know if they exist)

Present Perfect Subjunctive

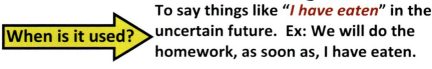

When is it used? To say things like "*I have eaten*" in the uncertain future. Ex: We will do the homework, as soon as, I have eaten.

Forming the Present Perfect Subjunctive:

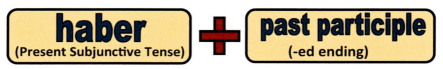

haber
(Present Subjunctive Tense)

+

past participle
(-ed ending)

Forming the Past Participle: See Page 93

haber: to have

YO **haya**	NOSOTROS/AS **hayamos**
TÚ **hayas**	VOSOTROS/AS **hayáis**
ÉL ELLA USTED **haya**	ELLOS ELLAS USTEDES **hayan**

Ejemplos:

Nosotros saldremos en cuanto ella **haya llegado.**

We will leave as soon as **she has arrived.**

Ella me ayudarás tan pronto como yo **haya comido.**

She will help me as soon as **I have eaten.**

Nos acostaremos cuando el partido **haya terminado.**

We will go to bed when the game **has ended.**

Imperfect (Past) Subjunctive
aka "The Cheerleader Verb Tense"

 **When is it used?**

To talk about wishes, doubts, emotions, etc. in the past.
Ex: *"I hoped that my parents would be happy."*

Often used with:
Past Tenses
Conditional Tense

Ra! Ra! Ra!

-ar/-er/-ir verb endings

YO	-a	NOSOTROS/AS	-amos*
TÚ	-as	VOSOTROS/AS	-ais
ÉL ELLA USTED	-a	ELLOS ELLAS USTEDES	-an

Forming the Imperfect Subjunctive:

Start with the infinitive verb	→	**Conjugate to preterite 3rd person plural (ellos form)** pg 61-62	→	**DROP -on**	→	**Add past subjunctive endings**

(yo)

estar → estuvieron → estuvier → estuviera

*The NOSOTROS form requires an accent on the final vowel before the "r": habláramos

Examples:

No había sido possible que fuéramos contigo.

It had not been possible for us to go with you.

Me gustaría que lo hicieras hoy.

I would like you to do it today.

Note: to say "there was/were" using the verb *haber* in the imperfect subjunctive, there is only one form: *hubiera*

Past Perfect Subjunctive

 To say things in the past that you had wished or hoped that had happened like *"I wished that I had eaten."*

Forming the Past Perfect Subjunctive:

haber
(Imperfect Subjunctive Tense)

past participle
(-ed ending)

Forming the Past Participle: See Page 93

haber: to have

In this tense, the first part of the sentence (the main clause) is either in the imperfect or the preterite tense.

YO	NOSOTROS/AS
hubiera	**hubiéramos**
TÚ	VOSOTROS/AS
hubieras	**hubierais**
ÉL ELLA USTED	ELLOS ELLAS USTEDES
hubiera	**hubieran**

Ejemplos:

Yo deseaba que <u>hubiera dormido</u> antes de la fiesta.
　　　I wished that I had (would have) slept before the party.

Yo dudaba que mis niños <u>hubieran limpiado</u> sus cuartos.
　　　I doubted that my kids had cleaned their rooms.

Yo esperaba que tú <u>hubieras venido</u>.
　　　I hoped that you would have come to the party.

"Si" if/then Clauses

To say <u>uncertain things</u> like "If this [thing happens] then [this other thing would potentially happen]"

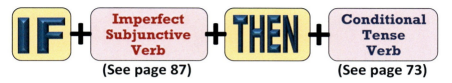

IF + **Imperfect Subjunctive Verb** (See page 87) + **THEN** + **Conditional Tense Verb** (See page 73)

Si (yo) **fuera** tú, **estudiaría** más.
If **I were** you, **I would study** more.

Si (yo) **tuviera** tres dólares, **compraría** un refresco.
If **I had** 3 dollars, **I would buy** a soda.

Si (yo) **pudiera** ser una persona famosa, **sería** Shakira.
If **I could** be a famous person, **I would be** Shakira.

Si (yo) **pudiera** vivir para siempre, **viajaría** más.
If **I could** live forever, **I would travel** more.

Si **hubiera podido ser** alguien famoso, **habría sido** Luis Fonsi.
If **I could have been** anyone famous, **I would have been** Luis Fonsi.

Si (yo) **tuviera** dinero, **viviría** en una casa muy grande.
If **I had** the money, **I would live** in a big house.

Si (tú) **estudiaras**, tú **sacarías** buenas notas.
If **you studied**, **you would get** good grades.

Compound Verb Tenses

(Progressive & Perfect Tenses)

The perfect tenses are used to express have/had/will have/would have _____ed (ex: worked). The progressive tenses are used to express ongoing actions using the "ing" form of the verb (example: working).

Present Progressive Tense

Forming the Present Progressive:

estar (Present Tense) **+** **gerund** (-ing ending)

Forming the gerund:

er/ir verbs → come~~r~~ } take off -ar, -er, -ir ending { add -iendo = **comiendo** (eating)

ar verbs → habla~~r~~ } { add -ando = **hablando** (talking)

estar: to be

YO		NOSOTROS/AS	
estoy		**estamos**	
TÚ		VOSOTROS/AS	
estás		**estáis**	
ÉL ELLA USTED	**está**	ELLOS ELLAS USTEDES	**están**

Ejemplos:

Yo **estoy haciendo** la tarea.
        I am doing the homework.
Ella **está abriendo** la caja.
        She is opening the box.
Nosotros **estamos durmiendo**.
        We are sleeping.
Ellos **están divirtiéndose**.
        They are having a good time.

Common Irregular Gerunds					
Infinitive	Gerund	Meaning	Infinitive	Gerund	Meaning
decir	diciendo	saying, telling	dormir	durmiendo	sleeping
pedir	pidiendo	asking	morir	muriendo	dying
repetir	repitiendo	repeating	poder	pudiendo	trying
sentir	sintiendo	feeling	leer	leyendo	reading
servir	sirviendo	serving	caer	cayendo	falling
venir	viniendo	coming	preferer	prefiriendo	preferring
freír	friendo	frying	traer	trayendo	bringing
reír	riendo	laughing	ir	yendo	going
seguir	siguiendo	following	construir	construyendo	constructing/building
mentir	mintiendo	lying	huir	huyendo	fleeing
vestir	vistiendo	dressing	influir	influyendo	influencing
creer	creyendo	believing	divertirse	divirtiéndose	enjoying oneself
oír	oyendo	hearing	despedirse	despidiéndose	saying goodbye

Past Progressive Tense

When is it used? ➤ To say things like "*I was eating.*"

Forming the Past Progressive:

estar
(Past Tense)
➕
gerund
(-ing ending)

Forming the gerund:

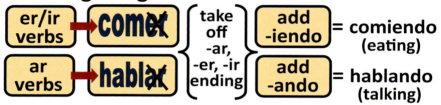

| er/ir verbs | → com̶e̶r̶ | take off -ar, -er, -ir ending | add -iendo | = comiendo (eating) |
| ar verbs | → habl̶a̶r̶ | | add -ando | = hablando (talking) |

estar: to be

YO **estaba**	NOSOTROS/AS **estábamos**
TÚ **estabas**	VOSOTROS/AS **estabais**
ÉL ELLA USTED **estaba**	ELLOS ELLAS USTEDES **estaban**

Ejemplos:

Estaba haciendo la tarea.
> I was doing the homework.

Ella estaba abriendo la caja.
> She was opening the box.

Nosotros estábamos durmiendo.
> We were sleeping.

Ellos estaban divirtiéndose.
> They were having a good time.

Common Irregular Gerunds

Infinitive	Gerund	Meaning	Infinitive	Gerund	Meaning
decir	diciendo	saying, telling	dormir	durmiendo	sleeping
pedir	pidiendo	asking	morir	muriendo	dying
repetir	repitiendo	repeating	poder	pudiendo	trying
sentir	sintiendo	feeling	leer	leyendo	reading
servir	sirviendo	serving	caer	cayendo	falling
venir	viniendo	coming	preferer	prefiriendo	preferring
freír	friendo	frying	traer	trayendo	bringing
reír	riendo	laughing	ir	yendo	going
seguir	siguiendo	following	construir	construyendo	constructing/building
mentir	mintiendo	lying	huir	huyendo	fleeing
vestir	vistiendo	dressing	influir	influyendo	influencing
creer	creyendo	believing	divertirse	divirtiéndose	enjoying oneself
oír	oyendo	hearing	despedirse	despidiéndose	saying goodbye

92

Forming Past Participles

To form –ed endings of words. Ex: tasted/jumped.

When are they used?
A past participle is a verb form <u>not</u> a verb tense and <u>cannot be used on its own</u>. The past participles are used with the verb haber as seen with the perfect tenses (pg 94-97). Ex: I have eaten ("eaten" is the past participle). Past participles can also be used as adjectives when paired with a noun or the verbs ser and estar. Ex: el juguete roto (the broken toy), el juguete está roto ([the state of] the toy is broken).
See page 47 for more examples of past participles as adjectives.

Forming the Past Participle:

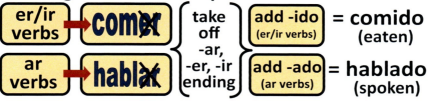

| er/ir verbs → comer | take off -ar, -er, -ir ending | add -ido (er/ir verbs) | = comido (eaten) |
| ar verbs → hablar | | add -ado (ar verbs) | = hablado (spoken) |

Past Participles with written accent marks with verbs that end in a vowel right before the –ar/-er/-ir ending:

caer	**caído**	fallen
creer	**creído**	believed
leer	**leído**	read
oír	**oído**	heard
traer	**traído**	brought

These verbs are <u>regular</u> past participles:		
ir	**ido**	gone
Ex: Ella ha ido. **(She has gone.)**		
ser	**sido**	been
Ex: He sido un mal amigo. **(I have been a bad friend.)**		
estar	**estado**	been
Ex: He estado muy cansado. **(I have been tired.)**		
tener	**tenido**	had
poder	**podido**	could

Common Irregular Past Participles		
Infinitive	**Past Participle**	**Meaning**
abrir	abierto	opened
decir	dicho	said
cubrir	cubierto	covered
escribir	escrito	written
freír	frito	fried
hacer	hecho	made/done
morir	muerto	dead/exhausted
poner	puesto	put/placed/positioned/well-dressed
resolver	resuelto	resolved/solved/determined
romper	roto	broken
satisfacer	satisfecho	satisfied
ver	visto	seen
volver	vuelto	returned

Present Perfect Tense

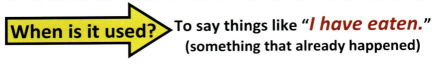

When is it used? ➤ To say things like "*I have eaten.*"
(something that already happened)

Forming the Present Perfect:

haber
(Present Tense)

➕

past participle
(-ed ending)

Forming the Past Participle: See page 93

haber: to have

YO	he	NOSOTROS/AS	hemos
TÚ	has	VOSOTROS/AS	habéis
ÉL ELLA USTED	ha	ELLOS ELLAS USTEDES	han

Ejemplos:

(Yo) he hecho la tarea.   **I have done** the homework.

Ella ha abierto la caja.   **She has opened** the box.

Ellos han comido el pastel.   **They have eaten** the cake.

Pluperfect Tense (Past Perfect)

 **When is it used?** To say things like
"I had already eaten."

Forming the Pluperfect:

 **haber** (Imperfect Tense) ➕ **past participle** (-ed ending)

Forming the Past Participle: See page 93

haber: to have

YO **había**	NOSOTROS/AS **habíamos**
TÚ **habías**	VOSOTROS/AS **habíais**
ÉL ELLA USTED **había**	ELLOS ELLAS USTEDES **habían**

Ejemplos:

Cuando llegó mi padre, yo ya <u>había hecho</u> la tarea.
   When my father arrived, <u>I had already done</u> the homework.

Ella ya <u>se* había duchado</u> antes de desayunar.
         <u>She had already showered</u> before eating breakfast.

<u>Habíamos hecho</u> la tarea cuando el programa comenzó.
         <u>We had done</u> the homework when the program started.

*Reflexive pronouns go **before** the verb haber in the sentence.

95

Future Perfect Tense

When is it used? To say things like *"I will have eaten."*

Often paired with the subjunctive mood

Forming the Future Perfect:

haber (Future Tense) ➕ **past participle** (-ed ending)

Forming the Past Participle: See page 93

haber: to have

YO		NOSOTROS/AS	
	habré		**habremos**
TÚ		VOSOTROS/AS	
	habrás		**habréis**
ÉL ELLA USTED	**habrá**	ELLOS ELLAS USTEDES	**habrán**

Ejemplos:

Cuando lleguemos al cine, <u>habremos cenado</u>.
　　When we arrive at the movie theater, <u>we will have had</u> dinner.

<u>Habremos hecho</u> la tarea cuando comience el programa.
　　<u>We will have done</u> the homework when the program starts.

Mañana a esta hora, <u>habré estudiado</u>.
　　　　By this time tomorrow, <u>I will have studied</u>.

96

The Conditional Perfect Tense

When is it used? **To say things like** *"I would have eaten."*

Forming the Conditional Perfect:

haber
(Conditional Tense)

past participle
(-ed ending)

Forming the Past Participle: See Page 93

haber: to have

YO		NOSOTROS/AS	
	habría		**habríamos**
TÚ		VOSOTROS/AS	
	habrías		**habríais**
ÉL ELLA USTED	**habría**	ELLOS ELLAS USTEDES	**habrían**

Ejemplos:

Tú <u>habrías hecho</u> más.   *<u>You would have done</u> more.*

Ellos <u>habrían querido</u> estar allí.

          <u>They would have wanted</u> to be here.

97

APUNTES (Notes)

APUNTES (Notes)

APUNTES (Notes)

APUNTES (Notes)

APUNTES (Notes)